THINKING COP

FEELING COP

A Study In Police Personalities

Stephen M. Hennessy, Ed. D.

Published By
Leadership, Incorporated of Scottsdale
7418 East Helm Drive
Scottsdale, Arizona 85260

ACKNOWLEDGEMENTS

As the case with anyone writing about the MBTI or psychological type for that matter, profound appreciation must be expressed for the work and wisdom of Katherine C. Briggs and Isabel Briggs Myers, in bringing Carl Jung's theory to life, along with the numerous scholars and practitioners who have, through their research with the MBTI, helped make some sense of this complex world of trying to understanding each other.

Appreciation must also be expressed for Dr. Mary H. McCaulley, Gerald P. Macdaid, and the many professionals for their diligent work with The Center for Applications of Psychological Type located in Gainsville, Florida. The non profit Center was established in 1979 to offer a variety of services to further the understanding of psychological type. Among it's many functions, the Center serves as a central repository for data collected through the use of the MBTI and is analyzed for type differences in occupations, age, and educational levels. The statistics from the several occupations compared to the data discussed in this book from the law enforcement profession was obtained from that data bank. I am indebted to the Center and those professionals. I urge those of you using the MBTI in the criminal justice area to share your findings with the Center. The more information the Center has reflecting our occupation will serve to deepen our understanding of the men and women in our profession and assist us in meeting the challenges of the future.

I would like to express my personal appreciation to the many police executives who willingly gave of their time to contribute to the contents of this book. Of those many professionals, I would like to specifically thank my good friend and professional colleague Thomas L. Reding, a Deputy Chief of the St. Paul, Minnesota Police Department, for his intellect, insight, and direction. Hobart M. Henson, Director of the National Center for State and Local Training, Federal Law Enforcement Academy, Glynco, Georgia, a former Deputy Director in the Illinois State Police, was the mentor who introduced me to the MBTI and to other issues on leadership, which ultimately made this book possible. Additionally, I greatly appreciate the encouragement and interest in my research on these leadership issues afforded me by a Minnesota law enforcement leader, Paul J. Tschida, former Commissioner of Public Safety, as my boss, associate, and friend for many years. Patricia Kelly, Management Course Director, Illinois Police Academy, also offered me valuable insights into this exceptional management tool throughout these past several years. Harry Halden, Mark Shields, and Jack Erskine, along with many others, all helped shape the information offered in this book.

I would also like to express my appreciation to several of my colleagues in academia, Dr. F. Barry Schreiber, Professor of Criminal Justice, St. Cloud State University, St. Cloud, Minnesota for his insight, friendship and support, and to Dr. Don LaMagdeleine, Associate Professor at the University of St. Thomas, St. Paul, Minnesota, whose constant challenging insured a strong academic base to my findings.

to my children,

Dawn and Nathan,

who every day remind me of

the importance of understanding, loving, and valuing

the differences in our lives

TABLE OF CONTENTS

®The Myers-Briggs Type Indicator is a registered trademark of Consulting Psychologists Press, Inc.

PREFACE

Six years ago, I had an opportunity to attend one of Steve Hennessy's leadership classes, which had become the regional management classes to attend if you wanted to learn something. In one of the courses we were divided into groups of five and worked together for one intense week on leadership techniques. I was fascinated in that, as the week passed, the group seemed to work exceptionally well together. Each participant's strengths and weaknesses seemed to match other group member's abilities as we worked through complex leadership strategies. After the class we all commented on the fact we had all worked so well together and Steve told us he had used the Myers-Briggs Type Indicator to assist in making up the groups. He had placed differing cognitive styles together to bring a variety of strengths into play as we worked with our problem scenarios. He believed that one primary reason we functioned so well together was these differing abilities complimented each other during our discussions.

With this concrete example of the usefulness of the Myers-Briggs Type Indicator, I became a believer and a student of the indicator. Finally, I was able to better understand why my chief functioned as he did, and why the quickest way to lose his interest was to bury him with details of a project. I was able to understand why, as a young patrol officer teamed up with an older veteran whose style of operating was so vastly different from mine, that our strengths seemed to compliment each other so that we functioned very effectively as a team.

During the past years, I have closely followed Steve's research and have prompted him at every opportunity to publish it into a pragmatic, easily read book for police executives and others who are interested in developing their leadership skills in working with others. Finally, a book that explains why dealing with some people seems to drive you crazy, while dealing with others is almost like being able to read their mind. Finally, a book that can explain why the media, politicians, and others in the helping professions can be so difficult to read and are usually so very different from the people in your law enforcement agency. The understanding you can gain from this book will help put these and other internal personnel issues into a new and different perspective.

I truly believe this book is an important addition to every police executive's knowledge base. We all need every tool we can possibly lay our hands on as the role of leadership becomes more and more complex.

Read this book for enjoyment. Its easy to get through. You will recognize situations we all see in our lives as law enforcement officers. Many of them are humorous and some of them are sad. Look at it hard, though, a second time as a new understanding of how people function that will assist you in dealing with others in your personal life and professional career.

Thomas L. Reding
Deputy Chief of Police
St. Paul, Minnesota

INTRODUCTION

Law enforcement systems occupy a unique position in our society. They represent a source of power that is not readily understood by many individuals. Agencies play a critical and necessary role in the preservation of public safety, maintaining public order and enforcing the law. Police officers have often been the target of widespread complaint and criticism, particularly in recent years. Police officers have been characterized as being cold, condescending, matter-of-fact and without compassion. They seem to be often at odds with the news media, social workers and correction's personnel.

The use of the Myers-Briggs Type Indicator (MBTI) can help in understanding why police officers may act as they do. The MBTI can assist police managers to better understand the different ways their employees approach problems and the various strengths they bring to the profession. It also can be used to help understand why some police personnel function better in certain jobs than in others and why some officers seem to be poorly suited for the occupation of policing. It can offer insights into why police personnel look at crime and violators differently than many social workers, defense attorneys, representatives of the media, and psychologists.

As an assistant director of the Criminal Apprehension Division of the Minnesota Department of Public Safety, I had occasion to conduct numerous training classes utilizing the MBTI. The class attendees were middle, upper and top level law enforcement officials from various sized police and sheriff's departments. Observing and studying the results offered many insights into the behavior of individuals who have chosen law enforcement as an occupation. The Myers-Briggs Type Indicator opened a whole new way of learning about the behavior of police officers.

As law enforcement executives realize, a law enforcement agency's most important asset is its employees. Agency leaders have a clear need to understand how their employees function on the job, and how they work best while involved with the many tasks of policing.

Recruiting individuals for job functions related to policing is a continual challenge. Intelligence, job interest, and physical agility tests, as well as personal interviews, are all used in various combinations. Recruiting efforts, however, may still target the wrong individuals for the job, or an individual may enter a profession and later realize that it was not the job they believed it to be.

In addition to recruiting, the functions of training and motivating police officers are critical. Police agencies have a responsibility to understand the reasons for lack of motivation, low productivity, transfer and attrition rates, and poor performance among police personnel.

Prior to retiring I was involved in the law enforcement profession for over twenty-five years. As all police executives know, being a law enforcement manager immersed in the daily happenings of the profession offers a unique insight into how people behave in the occupation. In the last several years, I taught numerous law enforcement leadership classes using the Myers-Briggs Type Instrument to facilitate communication and to point out differences in perception and judgement in team-building exercises. I administered the instrument to 286 police executives, ranging in rank from sheriff or chief to staff sergeant, and became extremely interested in the way Jungian Typology was reflected in the way they performed in the field.

As a way to look at performance, I interviewed 33 police executives, with nine holding the rank of chief or agency head, four deputy chiefs, seven captains or the equivalent, seven lieutenants, and six sergeants. The average length of service within the group was 20 years. At the time of the interviews, most of these individuals had occupied mid-to-upper supervisory ranks in their respective organizations. Of the thirty-three interviewed, one was an attorney, one had a master's degree, and one was a doctoral candidate. The average level of formal education beyond high school was 3.4 years. Twenty-two had bachelor's degrees and only four had no education beyond high school. All those interviewed were male except for one. She had the equivalent rank of captain in a police agency.

I was primarily interested in how those who shared Myers-Briggs Cognitive Styles, uncommon to the profession as described in Chapter One, had fared in the occupation of law enforcement compared to those who shared common types of perception and judgement characteristic to the profession. The issues I was interested in were:

1. How did the officer become interested in law enforcement?

2. What was the officer's first set of duties and what did they like to perform and perform well?

3. What tasks could they perform, but didn't like to perform?

4. Details of their career such as promotions, managerial style, strengths and weaknesses.

5. Did some officers feel or assume they were different from other police officers?

The conclusions in this study offered some fascinating views into the police profession through Jungian Typology.

Many of the comments in this book were taken from that research. During the compilation of the data, I promised confidentiality to those executives who participated in the interviews. To accomplish this, I modified the source of the comments to reflect slightly different ranks, organizations, and locations. As an example, a police executive from a southern community may be listed as coming from a northern community, a captain may actually be a lieutenant in reality. I did not change, however, rural or urban settings, nor the general size of the command or department. For those of you that participated in the study and read this book, I'm sure you will recognize your contributions.

The study of law enforcement through the use of Myers-Briggs cognitive styles can help executives in the profession understand their personnel better and can give those individuals outside the profession insights into why police perform as they do. For the cop on the beat, understanding different ways their co-workers and others prefer to take in information and make decisions can help them deal with those differences better.

This book is written for police executives, the officer on the street, representatives of the media, and other individuals involved in the field of criminal justice, to gain additional insightful knowledge into the complex world of law enforcement. Because of the varied backgrounds of those who wish to expand their knowledge on police personality, the book has many facets. To the police administrators, the chapter on the police profession will be elementary and simplistic. It has been included to re-draft what the occupation is really about from a lay person's point of view. The chapters on Jung's theory and the development of the instrument may be complex to some, but are included to explain how MBTI cognitive styles function in individuals. In your readings, I hope you will enjoy some of the insights it has to offer about the ways people deal with one another.

CHAPTER 1

MYERS-BRIGGS TYPE INDICATOR

Carl G. Jung, a Swiss psychologist, was a contemporary and associate of Alfred Adler and Sigmund Freud. Jung observed great disagreements between Freud and Adler in their understanding of the causal aspects of neuroses. The actual substance of the disagreements are unimportant here except that Jung, in examining the two points of view of both Adler and Freud, found them to represent an attractively simple polarity, which he considered an interesting phenomenon.

He found it interesting that two people from the same basic background and environment could approach an issue from two completely different points of view, when current scientific thought generally held that personality was much more of a product of environment than inheritance. Contrary to the thinking of the day, Jung felt that one's psychological type primarily was a product of genetic factors and that at birth the determinant of the way a person preferred to function in the world was formed. To this day, scientists and psychologists still debate the issue

1

of whether "nature", which would mean inherited characteristics, or "nurture", meaning the forces of the present environment, have more to do with the development of personality. One would assume that it is a combination of both factors that make up the personality of an individual. An interesting thought about the effect genes may have in personality development, however, may lie in a question one could ask a mother of two children born nine months apart, same sex, with the same father and mother, same environment, with the same socio-economic factors. If asked, she will usually comment about her sense that both children were completely different from each other only days after birth of the second child. In 1921 Jung wrote a book called Psychological Types that explained this theory.

The Four Functions:

Jung identified four basic functions which serve as a structure for an individual's personality.

Jung believed people perceive information in two ways, either through their five senses called ("Sensing") or through the sixth sense or ("Intuition"). According to Jung, people naturally have a preference for the use of one over the other. The more a person uses a function the stronger that function becomes, and the individual becomes more comfortable in using that specific preferred function. After accessing this information (Perception), a decision must be made based on the information, which is called making a (Judgement) about the information. Jung felt this was accomplished through one of two ways, deciding through the use of pure logic, called "Thinking", or through the consideration of social value affecting those around the decision, or the "Feeling" function. Jung felt these functions were an integral part of a person's personality which resulted in certain patterns of behavior which could be classified. The possible combinations of Perception and Judgement, according to Jung, were Sensing with Thinking (ST), Sensing with Feeling (SF), Intuition with Thinking (NT), and Intuition with Feeling (NF).

The Perceptive Functions: Sensing or Intuition

In Jung's system, individuals experience the world through Perceptions. He considered the perceptive functions (Sensing and Intuition) non-rational or irrational because the perceptive functions see things as they are, without the benefit of evaluation, which comes later during the decision making or Judgement function. The Sensing function sees sizes, shapes, colors, hears sounds, and employs the five senses during Perception. This function generally sees only what exists at the immediate time. People who use this function are usually considered to be practical, observant, realistic, systematic, and grounded in reality.

The intuitive function, on the other hand, sees things by way of a more generalized global way, being less aware of specific details. The use of Intuition gives the individual a general impression of a situation and also a sense of where it may be leading, and what may become of it. People who use the intuitive function are typically more involved in creative ventures such as planning, research, and strategic issues. The preference for the use of one over the other can be visualized as being on a continuum, with Sensing at one end and Intuition on the other as illustrated.

Sensing _____ Intuition

Jung felt that the preference for one over the other was "constitutional" or occurring at or near birth. One way to understand the preference issue better is to have a person take a pen or pencil in their dominant hand, usually the right, and to sign their name. Then, transfer the pen or pencil to their less dominant hand, usually the left, and write it again. Many will groan and complain or laugh at the effort it takes and some will say they can't do it. Of course they can, even though it usually does not appear as well written as when the dominant hand was used. This little exercise can illustrate how inborn preferences become stronger with use and those less used, not as well developed. Jung stated that people have a preference for a particular way of perceiving something, either through Sensing or Intuition. He said that when we use that preference over and over again, we become more familiar with that preference and more confident with its use. Most of us fall within the continuum, with one preference stronger than the other.

Typically, if people prefer the Intuitive function over the Sensing one, they concentrate on the total picture, but may tend to miss detail. On the other hand, if people perceive in specific detail, they tend to overlook the total picture. Since these functions are logical opposites, and to the degree that the Intuitive function is the superior function, the Sensing function will be proportionally weaker. The reverse is also true.

The Judgement Functions: Thinking or Feeling

Jung believed that the information assessed through Perception undergoes a distillation process on which an individual can make assessments for taking action. He termed this process a "rational" function.

Jung also believed that people make decisions through one of two preferred functions, Thinking or Feeling, as the continuum below illustrates.

Thinking   Feeling

Making a decision through Thinking about a situation requires removing oneself from its direct experience since Thinking involves a step by step process of understanding the situation in more objective terms. "Feeling", on the other hand, employs a process of reasoning, which takes it one step away from the reality of the experience to the subjective realm. Feeling means coming to a point of view about a situation more as a participant than an outside observer. It is not only perceived, but a judgement is made about it; one feels that it is acceptable or unacceptable, agreeable or disagreeable, delightful or not so delightful.

To the extent that a person thinks through a situation logically and comes to a sense of its meaning, the functioning has been neutral and non-judgmental. But, when that person responds to a situation with emotion and comes to a Feeling response, an evaluative position has been taken and cannot be neutral.

Jung felt that Thinking and Feeling were also mutually exclusive as is the case with Sensing and Intuition. If Thinking was a dominant function, Feeling would be an inferior function. If the Feeling function was the dominant function the Thinking function would be the inferior function. The dominant process for evaluating information became, along with the extraversion - introversion preference, the basis of Jung's Psychological types.

The Attitudes of Extraversion and Introversion:

Jung further theorized the existence of "Introverted" and "Extraverted" personalities, which he called "attitudes". Extraverts typically use their preferred functions in interaction with others, while Introverts are more comfortable checking the information obtained against their inside world of thoughts and ideas. When we talk about Introverts and Extraverts we are not talking about sociability. I know many Introverts that are very social and many Extraverts that are relatively quiet individuals. The director of training for a large police organization was a strong Introvert as measured by the MBTI, and Extraverted all day as an instructor and manager. He did, however, prefer to conceptualize internally by himself rather than externally with his staff. Because the main focus of my research was to look at the way uncommon types functioned in the police profession, I did not specifically look at the interaction of Extraverts or Introverts. As I interacted with both Introverts and Extraverts, I was concerned with the way they communicated their ideas about their occupation with the words and descriptions used, not in the way they formulated the ideas, externally or internally. If they introverted the ideas, I would just wait as they thought about the questions asked and then responded. If they Extraverted the response, I would just banter back and forth as they formulated the ideas verbally.

June Singer, a Jungian psychologist, studied Jung's work extensively and in her 1973 book *Boundaries of the Soul* stated that Jung described the Introvert as one who perceives in symbolic forms and is directed primarily toward internally understanding what is seen. The Introvert's interest in self-knowledge prevents being overpowered by the influence of outside, subjective surroundings. The Introvert deals with internal thoughts and concepts and defends against external intrusions. Introverts set themselves and the subjective psychic process above achievement in the public domain.

The Extravert, conversely, seeks means of expression outside. An object, externally to oneself, appeals intrinsically to the Extravert and captures the focus of interest. As a result, the Extravert has a tendency to abandon concern for self to concern for others. The Extravert is more socially oriented and seeks recognition from others as a predominant value.

Isabel Myers, the educator who developed the MBTI and Dr. Mary McCaulley, another researcher, educator, colleague and friend of Myers, founded the Center for the Application of Psychological Type. They wrote that even though some individuals dislike the idea of one process being more dominant and prefer to think of themselves as using all functions equally well, Jung held that such impartiality, where it actually exists, kept all of the processes relatively undeveloped and produced a "primitive mentality", because opposite ways of doing the same thing will interfere with each other if none has a priority.

The Auxiliary Process:

To understand how the functions work with each other during our daily lives, we need to understand the way the perceptive and decision making (Judgement) functions work together. When one function is dominant, the other one it works with is the auxiliary process.

If the dominant process is a judging one (Thinking or Feeling), the auxiliary process must be a perceptive one (Sensing or Intuition). Likewise, if the dominant process is a perceptive process, obviously the auxiliary needs to be a judging one. As an example, if a person's dominant function is a perceptive one of Intuition, the auxiliary function must be a Judgement function of either Thinking or Feeling. Logically it cannot be another perceptive function as the information has already been perceived though Intuition. Besides serving as a supplement to the dominant process, the auxiliary serves as a balance between Extraversion and Introversion.

For Extraverts, the dominant process habitually monitors the outer world of people and things, while the auxiliary process involves the inner world of concepts and ideas. For Introverts, on the other hand, extraversion must be accommodated to a considerable extent whether they want it or not. Paralleling the Extraverts, their dominant process dwells in the inner realm while extraversion is left to the auxiliary. But if the Introvert's auxiliary process is not adequately developed, the outward appearances and lives of the Introvert will appear very awkward, accidental, and often uncomfortable.

The issue of dominant and auxiliary processes creates an interesting twist in how Introverts are perceived by others. When dealing with an Extravert, the dominant process, inasmuch as it is Extraverted, is visible and conspicuous. As an example, when an Extravert is asked a question, they will usually respond immediately, as they prefer to use their extraversion in the process. As they talk, they are Thinking through the answer while they are talking so they may appear to change their minds as they go through the process. Their most trusted, most mature way of using their minds is immediately apparent. With Introverts, the reverse is true. Their dominant process is not readily apparent, since they are communicating with the outside world through their auxiliary. They will conceptualize in their minds before speaking and that is why they may appear to be more "quiet" or "deliberate".

Development of The Myers-Briggs Type Indicator:

Katherine Briggs, an educator, became interested in similarities and differences in human personality during World War I. She began to develop her own typology, largely through the study of bibliographies. During her research, she discovered the existence of Carl Jung's theory on personality types, which she began to explore and elaborate on.

Katherine was married to Lyman Briggs, a versatile scientist, who was the director of the National Bureau of Standards. He was a forerunner in the development of modern aviation and atomic energy, in addition to an explorer of the stratosphere and the continent of Antarctica. They had one child, Isabel, who entered Swarthmore College at age 16 and graduated first in her class in 1919. Having long been interested in her mother's work in Jungian typology, she was determined to develop an instrument to define and make the theory of practical use.

Isabel Myers began the task of developing an item pool that would tap the attitudes, Feelings, Perceptions, and behaviors of the different psychological types as described by Jung. For years she researched and tested numerous students as to preferences as she developed the instrument. The response to Myers' efforts from organized psychology was cool, if not hostile. The measurement of personality was considered a dubious enterprise by many psychologists, and among those few who were interested in personality theory and measurement, typologies were not in good repute. Trait and factor scales were the focus of research, and Myers' lack of established credentials (she was not a psychologist) didn't help to contribute to the acceptance of the Myers-Briggs Type Indicator (MBTI).

Myers' work did attract attention from a few assessment experts. Henry Chauncey, director of the Educational Testing Service, was sufficiently impressed with the instrument to approach Myers and offer to distribute the test for research purposes, which was done in 1962. During the next decade, several well known psychologists and researchers began using the instrument and writing about it. In 1975, publication of the MBTI was transferred to Consulting Psychologists Press, Palo Alto, California to allow for more widespread use. Also, in 1975, The Center for the Application of Psychological Type was founded in Gainsville, Florida by Mary McCaulley, Ph D., and Isabel Myers, as a research laboratory for the indicator.

The Design of The Myers-Briggs Type Instrument:

The MBTI is probably the most widely used psychological instrument for teambuilding and communications training in organizations today. In individual or group sessions, people can gain real insight into the ways individuals naturally look at issues from completely different points of view.

The instrument is exceptionally well researched, valid, reliable, and is non-judgmental in nature. It is intended for use with well people. The instrument is based on rich theory and is used internationally. As a matter of fact, the instrument is presently being translated into numerous other languages. Jung's theory on psychological types is generally assumed to transcend races, sexes and cultures as it deals with *the behavior of the human* mind.

The MBTI is a forced choice, self-disclosure instrument used to implement Jung's theory of type intended for determining basic preferences among normal personalities. It comes in three forms, Form F, Form G, and an abbreviated Form G. The four main dichotomies which typify personality are: Extraversion or Introversion, Sensing or Intuition, Thinking or Feeling, and Judgement or Perception. The various testing forms are Class B Psychological instruments and can be administered by persons who have extensive training in their use. The most common instrument used is Form G, which can be used in a training session with a few individuals. The Form G Abbreviated can be used in larger groups. This form can be self-scored by the attendees. The four polarities which the instrument measures are illustrated in Table 1.

Table 1. Four Principle Psychological Polarities

Preference For	A Person Focuses On
E-I E = Extraversion	The outer world of personal interaction
I = Introversion	or the inner world of concepts.
S-N S = Sensing or	Reality in what the senses know exist
N = Intuition	or relationships and possibilities by way of insight.
T-F T = Thinking or	To use pure objective logic instead of
F = Feeling	subjective merit and values of issues.
J-P J = Judgement or	To prefer closure and structure to flexibility
P = Perception	in dealing with the world.

After the instrument is administered, Table 2 illustrates some descriptors of the various combinations of preferences which constitute the sixteen types described by the MBTI. Each preference reflects certain characteristics that people of each type share. Everyone is an individual, but share the various preferences in each type category. People tend to act in ways that are most comfortable to them, which may or may not be the same as the ways others approach problems or situations. When this occurs, knowing about these different ways people function will go a long way in giving us insight to maintain good working relationships with others on the job. It is also useful to recognize differences in various, preferred ways of functioning that those in other occupations may use. We as law enforcement administrators can benefit by understanding the other ways people prefer to take in information and make decisions as we deal with them on a daily basis.

The following table reflects descriptors of the sixteen type preferences that make up the type table as used by the MBTI. The descriptors are from Sandra Hirsh and Jean Kummerow's *Introduction to Type in Organizational Settings* (1987). The table is divided into various columns linking like types together. The Thinking types are in the outside columns, the Feeling types in the inside columns. The table is split with the upper eight types being Introverts and the bottom eight types being Extraverts. The Sensing types occupy the right two columns of the eight descriptors and the intuitives occupy the left two columns. The judgement oriented individuals occupy the top and bottom rows with the perceptives in the middle. Below each of the sixteen types are adjectives that describe preferences generally exhibited by those sharing the functions.

Carl Jung felt that the center of our personality and how we are, was determined, to a large extent, on how we take in information and how we make decisions. These are called "functions" which involve the perceptive functions of Sensing and Intuition, and Thinking and Feeling. The combinations of these functions are Sensing-Thinking; ST

Table 2. Descriptors of Type Characteristics

Sensing Types		Intuitive Types	
Thinking	Feeling	Feeling	Thinking
ISTJ	**ISFJ**	**INFJ**	**INTJ**
factual	detailed	committed	independent
through	traditional	loyal	logical
systematic	patient	creative	original
dependable	practical	intense	visionary
realistic	organized	conceptual	theoretical
sensible	protective	sensitive	demanding
ISTP	**ISFP**	**INFP**	**INTP**
logical	caring	gentle	logical
realistic	sensitive	adaptable	cognitive
factual	observant	committed	detached
analytical	cooperative	creative	reserved
applied	loyal	devoted	precise
adaptable	trusting	empathetic	speculative
ESTP	**ESFP**	**ENFP**	**ENTP**
adaptable	enthusiastic	creative	enterprising
versatile	adaptable	curious	independent
energetic	friendly	versatile	strategic
alert	talkative	expressive	adaptable
pragmatic	cooperative	perceptive	resourceful
persuasive	outgoing	friendly	clever
ESTJ	**ESFJ**	**ENFJ**	**ENTJ**
logical	loyal	idealistic	logical
decisive	sociable	personable	decisive
direct	thorough	enthusiastic	strategic
practical	tactful	expressive	controlled
impersonal	responsive	diplomatic	challenging
structured	sympathetic	congenial	objective

Sensing-Feeling; SF; Intuitive-Thinking; NT, or Intuitive-Feeling; NF. The sixteen various personality types as measured by the instrument can be placed into the four combination of functions, called MBTI cognitive styles. For example, those types in the far left hand column, the ISTJ's, ISTP's, ESTP's and ESTJ's, are the MBTI cognitive style of ST, or Sensing-Thinking. The next column to the right, consisting of the ISFJ's, ISFP's, ESFP's and ESFJ's are the cognitive style of SF, or Sensing-Feeling. The next column, consisting of INFJ's, INFP's, ENFP's and ENFJ's are the NF, or Intuitive-Feeling cognitive style and the far right column, consisting of the INTJ's, INTP's, ENTP's, and ENTJ personality types, are the NT's or Intuitive-Thinking cognitive style.

MBTI Cognitive Styles:

The cognitive styles of NF, SF, NT, and ST are consistent with Jung/MBTI theory and fit well with current cognitive psychology. Current personality researchers recognize Jung's theory and the MBTI as cognitive style approaches. Cognitive processes include the ways in which humans process information and use their thought processes. Mary McCaulley, a founder of The Center for The Application of Psychological Type, has stated the foundation of type theory rests on the difference of taking in information and making decisions, hence the core of Jung/MBTI approach is the function combinations of NF, SF, NT, and ST, which are reflections of the cognitive process.

The information, comments and research reflected in this book are all based on the MBTI cognitive styles, which are the combinations of NF, SF, NT and ST.

CHAPTER 2

TYPE IN VARIOUS OCCUPATIONS

The Center for the Application of Psychological Type (CAPT), Gainsville, Florida, a research center founded by Isabel Myers and Mary McCaulley, maintains a data base containing the results of over 600,000 instruments indicating that certain individuals sharing common psychological types are attracted to various occupations disproportionately to the distribution of type in the general population. This data base is being added to daily by those individuals interested in how we function with one another.

There have not been any formal studies conducted with the expressed purpose in mind of determining a more exact estimate of the type distribution in the United States lately. The estimates in the following examples are the result of taking the numerous samples of those instruments on file at CAPT and extrapolating the following results.

Estimates of Frequencies of Types in the General Population:

Table 3 estimated percentages of various personality types in the general population in the United States.

Table 3. Estimated Type Distribution in the United States

Process	Percent
Extraversion..................	75%
Introversion...................	25%
Sensing.......................	75%
Intuition......................	25%
Thinking......................	60% Males, 40% Females
Feeling........................	40% Males, 60% Females
Judgement....................	55%
Perception....................	45%

This estimate was obtained from the results of Myers' sample of 12,860 males and 20,006 females, all of whom were eleventh and twelfth grade students from Pennsylvania. Several other estimates of the general population showed slightly less extroverts than Myers' sample above, but generally reflects similar distributions of type.

The CAPT sample population distributions are from data taken from samples generally collected in the United States from 1978 through 1982. It's interesting to note, however, that samples from individuals in various other cultures such as Japanese middle managers, Canadian consultants, Australian police officers, and English managers, when compared to their counterparts in the United States, generally reflect the same type distributions throughout the sixteen personality types.

The utility of population norms for researchers is that the distribution of types can differ markedly among different occupations. These differences can serve as a foundation for understanding the relationship between personality type and occupations.

Table 4. Normative Samples of MBTI Cognitive Styles.

N = 232,557

		Percent	Number
Intuitive-Feeling	NF	28.32	65,857
Sensing-Feeling	SF	29.34	68,233
Intuitive-Thinking	NT	17.56	40,841
Sensing-Thinking	ST	24.78	57,626
Totals		100.00	232,557

*Data Source:Macdaid, Gerald P., Mary H. McCaulley et al, (1986)

Cognitive Style Preferences in Occupations:

To illustrate that the distribution of cognitive styles can differ considerably from one occupation to another, I looked at four occupations outside the police profession that call for the use of different talents to perform the various job functions.

*Table 5. Managerial and Professional Bank Employees According to MBTI Cognitive Styles. N = 110

		Percent	Number
Intuitive-Feeling	NF	7.50	8
Sensing-Feeling	SF	27.10	29
Intuitive-Thinking	NT	7.58	8
Sensing-Thinking	ST	57.90	65
Totals		100.00	110

*Data Source: Macdaid, Gerald P., Mary H. McCaulley et al, (1986)

Managerial and Professional Bank Employees

Occupational tasks in the banking industry include those of counting money, balancing accounts at the end of each day, and keeping ledgers, among others. Additional daily tasks involved are computer operations, data typing, use of electronic posting machines, the need to write legibly, do simple mathematical tasks and other repetitive jobs. These tasks tend to focus on the immediate experience and require realism, acute powers of observation, memory and ability to deal with detail, and practicality, which is appropriate for those persons oriented toward the Sensing Perception. The tasks further reflect the need for analytical ability, critical and logical thinking, characteristics of those preferring the Thinking function of decision making.

As depicted in Table 5, the ST style is over-represented in this occupational group compared to the general population estimates, (57.90% to 24.78%) with the least represented groups being Intuitive-Feeling and Intuitive-Thinking. The job tasks in this industry would seem to include a majority of Sensing tasks, which are grounded in the present. The Sensing-Feeling group (27.10% to 29.34%) in the general population) represents general population norms and may reflect those persons involved in the public relations tasks of tellers and loan officers. Additionally, many deal with tasks using the five senses such as counting money, balancing ledgers and working with figures.

Small Business Managers:

The second group, represented in Table 6, the small business managers, reflects an even higher ST preference (70.6%). The NF percentage of 3.33% is greatly under-represented when compared to the general population (28.32%). Small business managers are involved in investigating and diagnosing problems using logical, analytical thinking in order to reach practical, sound conclusions. Logical thinking is essential when laying the groundwork. Interestingly, research has shown that one of the greatest causes for managerial failure is the inability to get along with others. This would makes sense if one considers the under-representation of feeling types (18.66%) compared to the general population norm of (57.66%).

Table 6.   Small Business Managers According to
MBTI Cognitive Style
N = 150

		Percent	Number
Intuitive-Feeling	NF	3.33	5
Sensing-Feeling	SF	15.33	23
Intuitive-Thinking	NT	10.67	10
Sensing-Thinking	ST	70.67	106
Totals		100.00	150

*Data Source: Macdaid, Gerald P., Mary H. McCaulley et al, (1986)

Table 7 reflects the MBTI preferences of Roman Catholic Religious Orders.   The ST function in this occupation is 10.64 percent, with the NF preference at 32.87 percent, almost the reverse of the occupations of banking and small business managers. The NF style, which is the dominant function in this sample, reflects the strengths of harmony, feeling, compassion, love, loyalty, and human insight. The occupations involving religious service call for unselfish concern, deference to others, maturity of spirit and a calling to help others.

Psychologists

Represented in Table 8 are members of the fourth group I looked at. Members in this occupation may spend time in research adding to our knowledge of human behavior.

*Table 7. Roman Catholic Religious Order Members According to MBTI Cognitive Function N = 2,002

		Percent	Number
Intuitive-Feeling	NF	32.87	658
Sensing-Feeling	SF	49.45	990
Intuitive-Thinking	NT	7.04	141
Sensing-Thinking	ST	10.64	214
Totals		100.00	2,002

*Data Source: Macdaid, Gerald P., Mary H. McCaulley et al, (1986)

The occupation of psychology deals with understanding human behavior, solutions to problems in human relations, and assisting with personal adjustment. The locations of the work sites, e.g. medical professions, academic institutions, and various types of private counseling contexts, however, constitutes a wide continuum.

Medical and counseling psychologists, for example, focus on healing the human psyche. Industrial psychologists concentrate on trying to make the work place better for people. Conceivably, if one were study this group in more depth, the majority of Intuitive Feeling types in this profession operate as clinicians in these contexts.

Table 8. Psychologists According to MBTI
Cognitive Styles. N=289

		Percent	Number
Intuitive-Feeling	NF	49.83	144
Sensing-Feeling	SF	8.30	24
Intuitive-Thinking	NT	30.80	89
Sensing-Thinking	ST	11.07	32
Totals		100.00	289

*Data Source: Macdaid, Gerald P., Mary H. McCaulley et al, (1986)

On the other hand, those who conduct research in either medical or academic settings may account for the Intuitive Thinkers among psychologists. Certainly the types of training and skills they need in order to conduct experiments, analyze them, and write up the results, emphasizes the rational synthesis of information characteristic of the preference for intuitive Thinking.

As you can clearly see, various individuals exhibiting specific cognitive styles congregate in certain occupations, those whose specific tasks call upon certain skills. People are obviously individuals and all types are represented in all occupations, however, by looking at the majority of cognitive styles in any one occupation, you can make an educated guess at the skills required for that occupation.

Uncommon Cognitive Styles:

Even though the majority of people in one occupation share the same cognitive style, one can find others in the occupation who are successful who don't share the cognitive styles of the majority. These are the persons we can call the uncommon cognitive styles in a occupation. Knowing how these people function becomes more and more important as we try to make decisions about work and the people who perform in our organizations. Knowing how the majority of people in law enforcement function, along with these "deviations from true north", becomes more and more important as our tasks become more specialized.

CHAPTER 3

THE LAW ENFORCEMENT PROFESSION

Police officers represent an anomaly in the United States. They are vested with an enormous amount of authority in a government founded under a system that generally dislikes and fears centralized power. The specific authority they possess to use force, detain, arrest, and search can be awesome in its effect on the freedom of an individual.

Yet, as a democracy, we are heavily dependent upon police to maintain the degree of order necessary to make a free society possible. Herman Goldstein, a scholar and police researcher, commented that police prevent people from preying on each other, provide a sense of security, facilitate movement, resolve conflicts, and protect the very process of rights such as free elections, free speech, and freedom of assembly on which the continuation of a free society depends. The strength of a democracy and the quality of life enjoyed by its citizens are determined in large measure by the ability of the police to discharge their duties.

The average citizen thinks of police work as primarily concerned with preventing crime and apprehending criminals. When crime increases, or a particularly heinous crime is committed, the public usually calls for more or better police personnel. Conversely, when crime declines in a certain area, the police often get, or try to take, the credit.

The real job of policing is far different from media portrayals in the newspapers, radio or on television. As stated by James Q. Wilson, a pragmatic, common sense professor of government at Harvard, the majority of calls have little to do with crime and a lot to do with medical emergencies, family quarrels, neighborhood disputes, auto accidents, barking dogs, minor traffic violations and similar events. Those calls that do involve actual felony crimes such as burglaries, robberies, and auto thefts, typically occur long after the event has taken place.

People today look on police as crime fighters, because this is an era of violent crime. The headlines of any newspaper are full of stories of violence that occurred the night before in any city in this country. The public demands protection! For various reasons, among them crowded conditions within the cities and the recent epidemic of cocaine, the crime rate in the United States has risen steadily the past fifteen years. Because we live with instant communications, news about crime arrives quickly via radio and television.

The flood of such news greatly heightens our awareness and concern about crime. We watch television cops who move in nonstop action for sixty minutes at a time (with appropriate breaks for commercials). On television a police radio report is received over the air and the officers speed through the streets (red lights on and sirens screaming), come to a tire-screeching halt, bail out of the cruiser (usually while it is spinning on its top after a spectacular crash), chase a violator down an alley into a dead end and either square off into a fight or pull him down from a chain link fence. The above poses an exciting and interesting plot line, but is generally inaccurate. Occasionally chases like this happen, but not to the extent the public may believe. As opposed to the media portrayal of police work, Charles Saunders, another police researcher, compiled a lengthy list of attributes and skills a police officer must have to perform the job of policing. These include the ability to:

1. Endure long periods of monotony during routine patrol, and yet react quickly and effectively to a problem situation on the street or to the radio dispatcher;

2. Gain extensive knowledge of the patrol area, not only the physical characteristics, but the normal routine of events, and the usual behavior patterns of its residents;

3. Exhibit initiative, problem solving capacity, effective Judgement, and imagination in coping with numerous and varying situations involved in a daily tour: a family disturbance, a potential suicide, a robbery in progress, a traffic accident, a medical emergency, or a disaster. (Police officers refer to this as having a lot of "common" or "street" sense);

4. Make prompt and effective decisions, sometimes having to do with life or death, and be able to

evaluate a situation quickly an take appropriate action;

5. Demonstrate mature judgement as to whether an arrest is warranted or not, whether to warn or scold, or be willing to take control and use any physical force necessary to control the situation;

6. Demonstrate critical awareness in discerning signs of conditions that are not ordinary, or circumstances that may indicate a crime is in progress;

7. Exhibit a number of complex psychomotor skills such as driving a vehicle in emergency situations, firing a weapon accurately under extreme and varied conditions, and maintaining agility, endurance and strength in taking an individual into custody while using the minimum force necessary;

8. Exhibit a professional, self assured presence and a self-confident manner in dealing with offenders, the public and the courts;

9. Be capable of restoring equilibrium to social groups such as mediating a family dispute, handling neighborhood problems, and dealing with street gangs;

10. Maintain objectivity when working with a host of special interest groups such as the press, family, victims, and offenders; and,

11.   Maintain a balanced perspective in face of exposure to the worst side of human nature.

These requirements are considered to be basic to the job of policing, regardless of the nature and size of the community policed. There are, however, numerous job tasks which are very important to the job of policing that involve not only the maintenance of public safety and order, but are important to the administrative functions of the department and to the image held by the public. These tasks relate to police and community relations.

As we know, the successful operation of a police department calls for the performance of tasks outside the general scope of the street officer.   Areas such as personnel, employee assistance, labor relations, planning and research, training and organizational development and recruiting, are also critical to the operations of the organization. In many instances, the skills called upon to perform these functions may differ greatly from those called upon for the performance of the typical street policing function.

Many of us know officers who perform satisfactorily on the street, but don't set the world on fire. We have seen these same officers receive an assignment in another area of the department and start performing like a star quarterback. If the tasks of both assignments were analyzed, we would find that they were vastly different. Because the individuals in question had an opportunity to use their natural strengths, they performed very well.

Being able to chart some of our strengths and possible weaknesses through use of the Myers-Briggs Type Indicator goes a long way in helping to understand why people sometimes don't seem to do well at some tasks and yet excel at others.

CHAPTER 4

POLICE PERSONALITY RESEARCH WITH THE MBTI

Concern with the quality of American policing and police dates back roughly to 1931 and the publication of the findings of the Wickersham Commission. This commission produced the first systematic explanation of the American criminal justice system. While the explanation centered on routine police practices, the report encouraged further research by people who today would call themselves criminologists.

The concerns and research seemed to focus in on what makes up a law enforcement officer; and in knowing how the officer may function, how can we better understand and direct police behavior? Scholars started to gather data, and gather they did! In the late 1950's through the early 1960's numerous studies were conducted into the profession. Peter Manning, a criminologist and researcher, listed over 78 various police research projects being conducted in 1976 alone, the era considered as the "Golden Age of Police Research".

It was interesting to note, however, that research on police personality involving the use of the Myers-Briggs Personality Indicator didn't surface until 1978.

Wayne B. Hanewicz was the first major researcher to publish his use the Jungian conceptual framework of personality types on the law enforcement profession. He used the MBTI framework to categorize various traits displayed by police officers into the sixteen descriptive quadrants defined by the Myers-Briggs Type Indicator. Hanewicz defined personality according to sociologist Thomas C. Gray's (1975) notion of affinity: *"... a predisposition to adhere partially to a set of distinctive sentiments that can be expanded and reinforced by training and socialization".*

Hanewicz interpreted previous research as reflecting two major positions: First, the police personalty is something police possess by virtue of being police, (i.e. job related) and, secondly, the police personality is something inherent in people who choose to become police officers. In the first case, "police personality" refers to a group of traits that are acquired after employment and is characteristic of the police profession alone. In the second case, "police personality" signifies a group of traits common to, but not exclusive of, police officers. Using this definition, a person who enters the police profession may share common characteristics with a person who enters another field which stresses some of the same traits needed to do police work.

Many researchers felt there was a personality exclusive to police, but Hanewicz disagreed, taking into consideration the Myers Briggs Instrument, Carl Jung's Theory, and other studies. Hanewicz and others felt there were possible overlaps between the personality required for police work and some other jobs.

According to Hanewicz, Jungian typology represented a promising approach to investigating the commonalities between police work and other occupations. He described a study undertaken with the Miami, Florida, police department in an attempt to improve police-citizen interaction. Determinants of police behavior were studied to understand the factors which influence police behavior and to relate them to police functions.

In the study, psychiatrist Jesse Rubin is quoted as saying, *"the type of people who enter police work are generally psychologically healthy and competent young men who display common personality features that should serve them well in a police career"*. He described them as generally restless and assertive, with a high level of physical energy. Further, their restlessness seems to derive from an aversion to introspection; rather, *"policemen look to the environment for perceptual stimulation in order to maintain alertness and optimal functioning"*.

Hanewicz also quoted a study of the New York City Police Department training activities, funded by the National Institute of Law Enforcement and Criminal Justice, which compared the value dimensions of police recruits entering the department in 1959 and again in 1968. He found a remarkable similarity among the personality traits valued by the recruits in both years, even though they were a decade apart. Alertness, job knowledge, honesty, dedication, and common sense were the top five of forty possible choices in the 1959 group, and were among the top six in the 1968 group.

Hanewicz's conclusions concentrated primarily on the predominance of certain personalty styles in the police profession and the fact these personality traits were shared by police along with those in certain other occupations. However, he only touched on the various possible organizational implications Jungian Typology suggests in better understanding the law enforcement profession.

In the 1980's several other researchers also examined police working personality through the use of the MBTI. Ron Cacioppe and Philip Mock, two researchers from Australia, conducted a study using a small sample of 191 senior Australian police officers regarding police self-actualization, quality of work experience and stress. Their personality type distribution, according to MBTI functions, resembled that of Hanewicz.

Another researcher, Ronald Lynch, who is with the Institute of Government at the University of North Carolina, conducted several studies involving the use of the Myers-Briggs Type Indicator. Like Hanewicz, Lynch found the distribution of the various Jungian Types through the police profession was much the same as the distribution Hanewicz found. Lynch also commented on the fact that the tasks of policing were also common to other occupations as well, such as in banking and engineering.

Hobart M. Henson, a Deputy Director with the Illinois State Police, conducted a comprehensive study utilizing the MBTI, seeking to develop criteria to help in recruiting persons especially suited to be police officers and to more effectively select, train, motivate and plan for growth in his agency. His data, drawn from a comprehensive sample of 2,114 veteran and recruit police officers, indicated the same general distribution of personality according to the MBTI as Hanewicz and Lynch.

I combined the distributions of various types obtained from the studies of Wayne Hanewicz, Hobart Henson, Ron Lynch, along with the study I conducted with three hundred police executives, and came up with a composite "Police Profile" according to Myers-Briggs cognitive styles. As one can see from Table 9, the least represented style in law enforcement is the Intuitive-Feeling (NF) cognitive style. The majority of police personnel clearly prefer the Sensing-Thinking cognitive style.

Table 9. Combined Police Studies According to MBTI Cognitive Styles. N = 3,101

MBTI Norms U.S. (%)		Composite Police (Mean) (%)	
NF	28.32	NF	6.3
SF	29.34	SF	14.0
NT	17.56	NT	16.6
ST	24.78	ST	64.1
	100.0		100.0
N = 232,557		N = 3,101	

Note that over 50 percent of the individuals who make up MBTI norms prefer making decisions (Judgement) with the use of the Feeling function, while only 20 percent of the police prefer making decisions in that manner.

Cognitive Styles and Police Officers at a Glance:

ST Police Officers

The vast majority of individuals in the law enforcement profession favor taking in information and processing it through their five senses and then deciding through the use of pure logic or subjective reasoning. General descriptors of the individuals preferring this way of functioning are: Concrete, Logical, Traditional, Organization-Oriented, Dependable, Decisive, Thorough, Duty and Service-Oriented, Observant, Practical, Matter-of-Fact, and Impersonal.

NT Police Officers

The second most common preference in the occupation, according to this study was the NT officers. They can be described as Goal-Oriented, Future-Oriented, Curious, Decision Makers, Precise, and Global. They tend to dislike detail and routine, and tend to sacrifice the present and look toward the future. They may forget specific detail and like to be involved in long range planning. Like the ST's, however, they make decisions through the use of pure, objective logic, which when communicating, makes them sound just like the ST's.

SF Police Officers

The third most common preference group in this study was the SF officers. These officers are typically Service-Oriented, Devoted, Friendly, and Optimistic. They are more interested in people than things, and tend to be sociable. These officers tend to focus on the concrete reality of the moment and are into detail. These officers, like the least common NF's, make decisions using social value and subjective considerations.

NF Police Officers

The group which comprises only five percent of the occupation, are the NF officers. They tend to be global, long range planners. They dislike detail, but enjoy people more than things. In the law enforcement occupation they tend to be the personnel-oriented individuals; the chaplains and employee representatives. My research reflected that many of these individuals held office in police labor organizations and preferred working in juvenile, community relations, and other, "people oriented" jobs. Of the seventeen NF's I interviewed, four had attended colleges and universities that specialized in pastoral or religious studies.

Being in the minority may cause some problems for them, especially for those with little seniority, as they may feel they don't really belong or are different from the mainstream officer, which, of course, they are.

The SF's and the NF's are the officers considered as "uncommon types" in the law enforcement profession, particularly because of their preference for "Feeling" as a Judgement function. They are, as one officer described himself, "a couple of degrees off of true north".

CHAPTER 5

CHOOSING LAW ENFORCEMENT AS AN OCCUPATION

One would assume we pick our occupations carefully The truth of the matter is that in most cases, we usually just "stumble" into an occupation which happens to suit us. If we look carefully back on our high school, early twenties, or early college years, we can see that we "tested" various jobs or tasks, quickly discarding or leaving those we didn't care for or weren't very good at. This "testing" was very subtle in nature, involving our study, our work and our play. Eventually, for the most part, we found ourselves in an occupation which seemed to fit us. Those of us that found ourselves in law enforcement enjoyed it and were good at it.

As has been stated, the ST's and NT's, those preferring pure logic as a Judgement function, comprise over 70% of all officers in the studies conducted by Hanewicz, Henson, Lynch and myself. The same was generally true of those in the Australia studies.

During the interviews in Minnesota, only three police executives could recall deliberately choosing law enforcement as the job they always wanted to have. The vast majority seemed to "just find themselves" there.

<u>The NF Cognitive Style and Entering Law Enforcement</u>:

All but one of the NF's in this sample did not plan to become police officers. The one officer who planned to enter the occupation was really interested in becoming a game warden, but was too far down on the hiring list. He subsequently was hired by a rural sheriff's department.

Basically I wanted to help people. At that time I wanted to conquer the world and help people. My favorite course in rookie school was first aid...I knew it would help me in my job...helping people. When I responded to an accident I knew I would need to know the stuff.

Another entered law enforcement between his undergraduate and graduate work. He was playing music at a saloon and got to talking with the deputy that was serving as a bouncer.

I was employed as a guitar player...studying sociology and psychology. I rode around with a deputy friend a bit and I liked it. I thought it was a pretty good deal. When I was sixteen I would pick up my girlfriend, put a buck's worth of gas in the Volkswagen and go drive down the back roads with the radio on. Now the county buys me a big fancy car with an Am-Fm stereo radio with the red lights and sirens and all kinds of toys to play with and air conditioning and I go down the back roads listening to the tunes. I don't have my girlfriend with me but what the hell... they buy the gas.

Another officer grew up in a lower middle class neighborhood where he liked and respected the police with whom he came in contact. That was in the days of beat cops on Lake Street and the park police, *"...and like I say, generally they would be very helpful, nurturing, good people. Now if I would had met the bad ones, I might have felt differently..."* He met several probation officers because of the nature of the neighborhood and the fact that some of his friends were in trouble with the law.

> *So that's the way I came into it. I thought this is a good job, this is where you can make a difference in society. Kind of a uniformed social worker I guess is how I looked at it.*

Several individuals, both now heads of their agencies, never wanted to get into law enforcement. One finished a double major in English and speech communications. Several of his good friends joined the police department as a way to get out of the draft. He had been urged to join as a way of getting out of going into the service, but really wasn't interested in the profession.

> *I wasn't going to be a cop. I didn't want to be a cop. So I got drafted. I did some AWOL apprehension while I was in the service...That was interesting and when I got out I thought a little bit about law enforcement, but I didn't want it for a career. I wanted to teach in college. My wife's father had been a cop and she told me she had no intention of being married to a cop...she said they drank too much...and always the half priced meals, the free coffee, 10 percent discount at stores, the whole image. So I looked around for a job and while at it, took the Fairfield City police test. They offered me a job...my wife was kind of upset about that, but I said, well it's different, it's a suburban department.*

The head of another large agency majored in business administration and earned a master's degree in Sociology.

When asked why he became interested in the profession he replied:

I wasn't. My dad was a cop, my uncles were cops, my cousins were cops and the last thing I wanted to be in the world was a cop. My aptitudes, as I was growing up, leaned more towards writing and history. I was a history major in college until it finally sunk in that if I wanted to make a living, I had better switch to something else. And still to this day, I don't know why I became a cop. I care a lot about people and I wanted to help people, I guess...

The SF Function and Entering Law Enforcement:

In the SF group, only two of those interviewed planned to become police officers. One stated *"well I determined in the sixth grade that I wanted to be a police officer and I never changed my mind through today."* The other said *"I guess I always was interested in police work from the time I was a teenager."*

The other six took the job because at the time it looked attractive.

"Originally I wanted to go in the seminary. Then I found out ya can't get married. Then I went from there to education...there wasn't a whole lot of opportunity in education without a high GPA, so I thought I should think about something else," said one. He spoke with a friend who was joining the St. Paul Police Department and decided to test for several other departments too. He applied for, and was accepted by, a major metropolitan police department. Another stated: *"I wasn't really looking*

for a career, I was just looking for an interesting job and the police department was hiring."

An SF, who later became the chief of a large police agency, happened to be looking in the paper one day and saw an advertisement for police officers in the help wanted section. Before that he had never had any desire to be a police officer but had always admired them.

As you can see, the vast majority of NF's and the SF's did not really plan to become police officers, as is the case with the NT's and the ST's. Notice also that the NF's and SF's primary communication pattern involves "people" and "helping people".

The NT Cognitive Styles and Entering the Occupation:

As with the NF's, SF's and ST's, the choice of policing as an occupation for NT's seemed to be more accidental than intentional.

An NT captain in a major metropolitan law enforcement agency, and a licensed attorney, became interested in law enforcement by chance. He enlisted in the army and picked jump school as a skill choice. He ended up in a military police group, was transferred to Germany and assigned to a local criminal investigative division. He enjoyed the investigative work and when he was discharged, he went home and took the police test. After joining the department he was assigned to work midnights on the west side. *"I enjoyed the freedom. I always thought of police work as "we were smarter than they were". Sometimes it was a matter of trying to be smarter than they were and catch them."*

He went back to school, completed his degree and then attended law school during the evenings. Shortly after graduating, he was assigned to research and development.

I liked the newness of it. I mean the projects we did. When you got an assignment, you had to create a way not only to get it approved, but to create a way to get it to work. The thing about research...as soon as you think you've got it all together, somebody else points up another problem...and afterwards you just adjust and react and solve them. Some things were unsolvable, there was no solution to them...but a lot of people I work for, or work with, want simple answers to very complex problems and there aren't any, so that was frustrating.

Another officer, an NT director of a law enforcement agency, "felt a calling" during seventh or eighth grade to become a police officer. He attended college and became a community service officer for a suburban police department, and then became a licensed police officer for the same suburban department.

(I worked) everything from traffic accidents to burglary calls, domestics, emergencies...I couldn't stand to process a crime scene. Just that detail work, the idea of getting there and looking for fingerprints...that was just worthless. But I did enjoy things like traffic...thoroughly enjoyed doing traffic...traffic accidents. I went into school. Medicals and domestics were fun.

Comments like that above were rare. Most officers, no matter what their Myers-Briggs Cognitive Styles were, just seemed to fall into the occupation with not a lot of forethought.

A third ring suburban chief of police, an NT, commented about becoming a police officer:

"I was with the Vista project, that's Volunteers In Service to American. I was supervising the Vista project for the north and the south sides of Minneapolis. It was an interesting thing and I wanted to do something that was interesting with people."(This comment is unusual coming from an NT, but see the following comment about "social work".)

He became frustrated with the Vista project, dismissed some of his people and made some public statements that the project was not serving people as it should. *"Well I ultimately found out that social work in any form wasn't something I was interested in..."* In the early 1970's he spoke with a chief in a suburban police department who was starting a fairly unique program for policing. He joined that department. He was immediately attached to the detective division and developed a strong ability to work crime scenes for that department and for surrounding suburbs. After four years, he applied for and was hired as a chief of police in a smaller community.

ST's and Choice of Law Enforcement as an Occupation:

Interestingly, the ST's seemed to "fall into" the occupation without a lot of conscious thought, as was the case with the other styles. One ST, who rose to a rank of deputy chief stated, *"Quite honestly, I was looking for a decent job."*

Most of us would admit, even though we are in an occupation we really are satisfied with, the process of choosing that occupation appeared to be random. Again, what the vast majority of us do unconsciously, is try numerous tasks, quickly discarding those we don't particularly enjoy doing or don't do well. There are those officers who may have felt somewhat uncomfortable in this profession but could do the job. They didn't particularly like it, but stuck it out and survived for a myriad of reasons including security, pensions, and other benefits. I would bet their preferred occupational strengths, as measured by the Myers-Briggs Type Indicator, are probably in areas other than those strengths called for in the police profession.

CHAPTER 6

VARIOUS PERSONALITIES IN POLICING

During the three years I conducted these interviews, a real difference was noted between the far greater number of Thinking types (ST's and NT's) and the minority Feeling types (SF's and NF's) and the way each looked at and spoke of the tasks of policing. During conversations, NF's and SF's talked about people constantly, using many colorful descriptions of street characters, and using the word "people" or "persons" many times. The NF's and the SF's often spoke of their strong ability to communicate and relate to people on a personal level.

The use of the words people, folks, kindness, appreciation, and the like, are common in the conversations with Feeling types. The Thinking types, both NT and ST described things in more literal, general task terms. One ST deputy chief described his staff as *"uniforms and clerks"*. Similarly, an NT captain described his transfers in terms of tasks rather than in terms of people. The ST's typically discussed their jobs in the terms of performing tasks rather than the people encountered while doing them, while the NF's and SF's seemed to describe their occupations in the context of dealing with violators and describing their associates as individuals.

The NF's and SF's Dealing With People:

The prime concern of NF's while on duty was helping people. Their abilities were strongest in talking with and dealing with people. Note this comment from a NF deputy sheriff commander from a large metro sheriff's office:

My favorite calls were domestics. Back then there wasn't any domestic assault law so you just went in there and broke it up...it was kind of fun to go in and defuse the situation. I could talk to just about anybody about anything. I learned to like and still like an honest crook, a guy that makes his living being a crook. When you catch him he doesn't give you a lot of baffling bullshit...I mean periodically you run into somebody that there ain't any point to talking to, I then arrest his ass and throw him in jail. End of story.

Another NF commander of a large agency spoke of his experiences working in the early days in a rural area of southern Minnesota. The need for one to be able to talk their way out of a potentially dangerous situation in a friendly manner was a critical attribute:

Here in the city if you get into trouble you pick up the radio and you get help. My experience in the rural area was the best I ever had...it taught me so much that you have to talk to people. You learn that when a big Dutch farmer is drunk and he tells you he doesn't want to go to jail and to take him home and come pick him up Monday morning and we'll go to court, you can trust him and believe him. Here (in the city) you'd have more of a tendency to slam him up against the trunk and throw the cuffs on him. If you did that down south at 2:00 am you would probably go home by yourself with your handcuffs in pieces.

Prior to this same director being promoted and assigned to his present command, he was transferred to a precinct which had a reputation of the officers getting in fights with violators much more frequently than in the other precincts. He commented on why he felt that was happening:

There's a reason the cops are being assaulted. Here the city's not that bad. We have some tough neighborhoods but any cop who is getting thumped a couple of times a week...there's a reason they are getting thumped...it's because of the way they may be treating people, in my mind. I just told them that it's no longer acceptable to treat people as less than human beings and if you do and you're wrong, I'm going to have your head. On the other hand, I'll stand right next to you if you do your job aggressively and right.

He commented that his complaint level was now down almost 40 percent, while the incidence of police injuries was down over 80 percent.

One NF lieutenant, working for a rural sheriff's office, talked about first coming on the department:

Yeah I didn't even own a gun, I didn't have a uniform. I borrowed a friend's uniform...the sheriff gave me his gun and holster and said, just don't shoot anybody, just drive along. Don't make any traffic stops unless someone runs into you.

He particularly liked the domestic calls in the rural areas. They tended to revolve around family problems such as the kid coming home drunk or the disputes between families:

They would say go take care of that guy and I'd roll down there and was able to talk my way through that...I was very comfortable talking and dealing with those folks. I guess I didn't feel I was any better than the folks I was dealing with on the street...the citizens. I could easily see where I could be in the same position as they were. You have to find a way to deal with these folks on their level. I didn't write a lot of tickets because I didn't have to. I would walk right up to the kid and say I'm going to be here night after night, and if I see you doing that again I'm going to write you up. That seemed to work for me. I gained a lot of respect from the kids that way. I know there are other, more creative ways of dealing with something other than just a black and white hard-assed police attitude. I always thought people were individuals, and that every situation was different. So I look for the difference in people and treat them with what the situation needs.

The police group representing the SF preference obviously shared many of the same social value and warmth considerations as the NF group.

For example, working in a poor neighborhood with a lot of minority group types, blacks and Indians, poor white people, a lot of welfare folks and stuff, I saw my job as really helping and serving and supporting these people. I would ride down the street and spend a lot of time waving at people as I went by and they would return the wave...or to stop at a playground and just talk to some kids in the field and stuff. I was more than willing to get involved in arrests and scuffles if it was necessary but the attitude of cops against the public and the public are the bad guys didn't wash with me. You can't treat people that way.

The next comment also reflects the concern for people or people orientation, as spoken by a commander in a rural sheriff's department:

The sheriff that originally hired me made the comment that he didn't care if it was a little old lady that had a cat piss on her porch. He wanted her contacted because that was the most, the single most important thing in her life at that moment. I think the theory is very good. In law enforcement, it's the contacts, even though the mediocre calls aren't necessarily exciting...you take care of them, and I think you gotta keep that uppermost in your mind...what are the people problems, and to deal with them.

To this deputy, the important part of the job involved treating people in an appropriate manner:

To me that's one of the biggest parts of the job. You gotta understand the citizen. You gotta have some feeling towards them and it can't always be negative. Just because they were going 70 in a 55 does not make them public enemy number one. I see the younger officers thinking that the speeders are bad, totally bad and I have a hard time handling that. I try to get it across to them that they are just citizens that we caught speeding. Maybe because of my nature I'm too far on

50

the other end of the spread, but I'm trying...my goal is to reach a happy medium.

Another example of general concern for people expressed by an SF came from an officer with twenty years seniority:

I went down and walked the beat near Douglas Avenue, which was our black neighborhood. I loved working down there. You had absolutely full latitude to do any kind of police work you wanted to and I liked the people and they liked me. It was a dream for a young policeman. There was all the police work in the world you could do. And fun type stuff. Old stuff like go to a crap game in the garage and run in and scream and watch them all go out the doors and windows and then you pick up the blanket with the money and dice on it and then walk down to the little old Black church and say to the administrator, here's a gift from the community for ya. Storybook stuff.

I just liked the people. They were fun. They were energetic, they were also involved in a lot of crime, too. It was a police officer's dream. I just went down there looking at it as a real opportunity to have a lot of fun doing police work and that's just what it ended up being...it was every street character in the world, pimps, whores, junkies, anything you wanted was there, and in those days, the beat man had a tremendous rapport with these people.

Another SF officer from the same department was a relatively large, quiet, man who really enjoyed his assignment with the juvenile division. He was assigned to the group for several years and was then promoted to lieutenant. He supervised the unit for another year and was then moved to internal affairs. He said his favorite assignment was working juvenile. He really liked working with the kids and would have been content to stay there for the rest of his career. He felt that one had a better chance of making an impact on kids than opposed to working with adults. His time in juvenile was limited though, and he was assigned to internal affairs and then to family violence. The cases he handled there were sex crimes such as rapes, exposures, child abuse, and domestics. He took the transfer to get out of internal affairs because he didn't like the adversarial relationship with his fellow officers but, he didn't like the family violence assignment at all:

It was a depressing place to work. Ya know, constantly handling child abuse cases and rapes and all that kind of stuff is hard work...emotionally hard. Ya know when you have to interview little kids about how they were molested by their father or what have you, it's not fun stuff for anybody. I would think my strongest point would be my concern for people. I don't know what term you would use, not necessarily a negotiator or counselor or anything like that, but I suppose when I was a detective I...had an ability to talk heated situations down as opposed to taking physical action right off the bat Of course sometimes it didn't work and you had to take physical action.

Another lieutenant, an SF from the same department, described his tour of duty in the jail of a major metropolitan department during the 1960's. His affinity for people is quite evident in the following excerpt:

No...it was horrible, it was like before the industrial revolution. It was a jail...a prison. We had people in there with communicable diseases...we had people in there that were so sick they were dying. I can remember the American Civil Liberties Union came over and forced (them) to come up and examine the jail. The poor guy never wrote a report...I think he went out of there so beat up because I told him...I have to work and live with these people every day. I take chances and give these people major medication to get them through because they are so sick. I give them alcohol, I give them anything to get them going because they are dying on me...I took the inspector back and they were like tiger cages. It was a jail built back in 1890. It had never been updated...it was a horrible year of my life.

Much the same concern for working in and among people exists in the rural areas. One 6 foot 3 inch, 225 pound SF officer stationed in a rural sheriff's office began his career on the sheriff's water patrol. His uncle had been the chief of police in his home town and his father had been a police officer. This SF had been a religion major in college and is now an ordained deacon in his church.

I didn't care for the serious car accidents...(because of my) feeling for people. When they were hurt and so forth it bothered...I did find it bothered me...And that was something I had to learn...learn to overcome and live with. The contact with people, I would say for the most part, was good and enjoyable and that's what I enjoyed. Trying to work out and work with them or their various problems. I've had a hard time with some officers who seem to think that it's us against them and view most situations in a black and white manner. Most

*of the folks we deal with are honest folks and are just
in a jam. They need a little consideration too.*

NT's and ST's and the Tasks of Policing:

According to Isabel Myers, NT's and ST's are generally
systematic and analytical, often to the point of being or
seeming impersonal. As we contrast the descriptions of
tasks and duties by NF's and SF's with those by ST's and
NT's (the majority of cognitive types in the law
enforcement profession) you can easily see the difference
in concern for people and concern for task.

Another example of this orientation is clearly reflected
by an NT captain of a major metropolitan agency. He
commented on walking a beat. Note that he never mentions
people in his description:

*Walking...I kinda preferred that. I had the opportunity
several times to ride what they called the district squad
in a car and declined. Wanting to work there in the
center of the action, so to speak. Something always
going on, variety that we always like, and lots of learning
in the center setting as opposed to, way, in a district out
in the far end of the city where you just didn't have
much exposure to policing activity.*

Contrast that description with the following colorful
quote from an earlier comment by an SF officer in the
same department.

*I just liked the people (on the beat). They were fun.
They were neat; they were energetic; they were also
involved in a lot of crime. There was every street*

*character in the world; pimps, whores, junkies... anything
you wanted was there.*

In a discussion about what they liked about police work,
one ST, who eventually became a deputy chief, stated *"I
had a lot of freedom. I really enjoyed the variety. You just
never knew what the next minute was going to bring. I
enjoyed that."* He further commented on working traffic:

> *I almost have to say that I enjoyed sort of the cat and
> mouse game, trying to catch them doing something, that
> sort of became a competitive type thing. I really kind of
> enjoyed, strange as it sounds, taking care of crashes
> where you can really dig into things and you can...I even
> liked doing first aid and things after I got through it, ya
> know, I didn't particularly like picking up dead bodies
> and stuff like that, but I had a few rewarding experiences
> by saving a few lives along the way.*

Another ST enjoyed the traffic aspect of the job,
although for him it was part of a larger fascination with the
adventure of police duties. He worked with a state agency
where the job was generally traffic-oriented, but, because
they were sworn, licensed police officers, they could
become involved in any law enforcement violation:

> *I liked the action, catching drunks, you could...being on
> the patrol is a great job even if you don't like traffic. As
> a trooper, you've got the ability to roll on anything you
> want, I mean, you can help other police departments
> and when action's over you don't have to do any
> paperwork. You can go in on armed robberies,
> kidnappings, or chases, or just anything you hear, ya
> know, with a scanner. You know what's going on all*

over the metro area. And the other coppers are always happy to have ya show, ya know, they don't feel that you're stealing their thunder. So it was a good job...

Another ST, a deputy chief of a large metropolitan department, again commented on the excitement and variety:

I started the job and found that it was extremely exciting...it was a huge challenge and the structure of the department was changing...I was offered three or four positions, I stayed in patrol only for a year or so and went to the former tactical squad (power shift) with the youngest charger on the department.

He was transferred to a special research project which involved teaching civics classes in the school system. He taught criminal justice studies to ninth grade students. The aim was to try to overcome some of the racial tensions and to stimulate understanding of the criminal justice system. He was then promoted to sergeant and assigned to school liaison:

I was out at Grant Junior High and Central High School which were...65 percent black. It was a challenge. It was like transposing street crime into the schools and obviously had the stabbings and the shootings and the drug problems way back then...again it was very challenging and very exciting.

As you can see from the comments, the focus of the ST's and the NT's is generally on the excitement and variety of the job, without any real comments about the people. An ST lieutenant working for a state agency was a water patrol officer, drove an ambulance, worked for a sheriff's department as a desk officer, patrol officer and jailer, and was hired as a narcotics investigator. He commented on narcotics investigations and working in the section:

I loved it...the challenge, the role playing, the opportunity to...everything, every situation was different as far as I was concerned. You had to try a different approach or use a different line or use a different role...it was a target type situation or a goal out there you had to achieve. It was never dull. It was never boring. It will always be the highlight of my career...enjoyment wise.

He moved from working undercover to organizing task forces and working complex drug cases. *"It was like putting a novel together, or pieces of a puzzle...it was really enjoyable".* He then transferred into the training area where he developed new courses for narcotics training.

As is the case with others sharing an ST preference, concern with task is evident in the above discussions of police work. In a several minute discussion of the various transfers this officer was involved with, the only time people were mentioned was the comment *"...you knew in your mind that the individual was a violator".*

This approach contrasts sharply with the comments by the SF chief of police in describing his task as *"...working in a poor neighborhood with a lot of minorities...I saw my job as really helping, serving and supporting these people and would ride down the street and spend a lot of time waving at people as I went by".*

CHAPTER 7

MANAGEMENT STYLES
AND HOW THEY MAY DIFFER

The NF Cognitive Style in Management:

You would assume that the typical NF style of management would be people-oriented and somewhat reflective in nature. This seemed to be the case with most of the individuals I interviewed. An NF street sergeant in a suburban department characterized his management style as follows:

I think I've sacrificed maybe some short term performance for a long term relationship where in critical situations you may get performance that you may not have had otherwise. Some people think they should be a hard-nosed supervisor and I think they get begrudging results...if they stay behind somebody and crack the whip. This job relies so much on independent performance that (you don't want them to be) out in a car thinking what a jerk their supervisor is. They (the supervisor) can't be everybody's best friend, but if you take the abrasiveness out of it...you get better performance. That's just my style...that's reinforcing the idea of letting people do their jobs and valuing their input and valuing their talents...so I've been luckier than a lot of the other supervisors with what I consider to be high performance people.

These interesting comments contain several elements characteristic of NF's. The "sacrificing short term performance" principle reflects the conceptual, future orientation of the Intuitives. It also legitimizes a generally supportive attitude toward people.

Another aspect of this managerial style is the premise that administrative power ought not be abused. From this perspective, *"they don't need a clock watcher, they don't need a baby sitter, and they don't need a slave driver."* One NF sergeant really resented his previous supervisor who timed lunch breaks, coffee breaks and was always hustling on the radio to see if he could catch someone doing something wrong. He commented about his attitudes on supervision:

It's January, it's 3:00 in the morning, 20 degrees below zero and you haven't seen a car on the road for two and one half hours. I don't care if you sit in a coffee shop for an hour because come July or August you aren't going to get a coffee break at all. And I believe that by the end of the year it's all going to wash out within five minutes, and I'm not going to lose sleep over five minutes and neither are you. And I would rather have you be open, and not try to be hiding things from me when you seriously have a problem. I want you to understand that I'm not being chicken shit and want you to understand that you can come to me first.

An NF police chief of a suburban department described his personal management style as emphasizing the service nature of the police role. He stated that the best cops he has and *"ironically the ones who also have the best enforcement record"*, are those who are the most service oriented.

Well, probably what I should do is send you a copy of our '89 goals and you'll see where we are. We are primarily service oriented. Basically the idea is that my number one goal is that no one should ever have to call us twice. That means that if they call we will meet their needs. And I've taken it far enough that if it isn't in our jurisdiction we will connect them to the right one. We won't send people away saying we can't do that...because once they've reached us they have their link. I think I have a very open department. It's participatory in the sense that everyone has a chance to be heard and participate. I'm not democratic by any means, but if somebody has a good idea and if we adopt it, we let them run with the idea whether they are a patrol officer, sergeant, or whatever.

Describing this same outlook differently, an NF captain in a large metropolitan agency commented, *"I'm a people person, that's my strongest asset"*. In his opinion, he considers a potential decision's implications for the people concerned with the decision, before considering anything else.

"To make black and white decisions without considering the people involved, I can't do, even though it would be easier if I could." This captain experienced a continual struggle with his superiors, which he felt typified an autocratic management perspective. He was friendly with people

downtown, but noted a distinct lack of people skills there. He merely hopes they will leave his precinct alone.

My people skills give me an extra dimension, but also it gives me more frustration because I'm dealing in a culture that historically does not consider the individual people involved...I've never been able to separate cold fact from the people involved. My philosophy is that we are all adults in an adult situation. You know the rules, you do the job. If you break the rules then I have to do something about it, but I'm not going to sit over you with my thumb. It seems to be working (management style)...I get the results that downtown is looking for. If I didn't get the results, though, I'm sure that management would think it's because I am more people oriented and in their eyes, not tough enough.

One can see in the conversational style of the NF's interviewed, that they used the words "people" often and seemed to be more oriented towards the individual. The same is true with SF's as well as NF's.

The SF Cognitive Style in Management:

The SF group represent their skills in dealing with people as their strongest managerial asset, as is the case with the NF group:

I feel that my approach is, let's find out what the problem is, approach that person, sit down with him or her and give them an opportunity to say what is or isn't. And that's where we (the feeling types) differ, because so many times my sergeants will go out and they'll blow off steam...it creates a real conflict in the department.

Another chief (SF) of a major suburban metropolitan police department commented:

You have to be sensitive to people's needs. I believe in a chain of command, but it can shut good ideas down...I think this whole issue of...there was a time when the boss came in and gave orders and the people did what they were told or lost their jobs...that's not a creative atmosphere in which to work...you need an environment where you can make good faith mistakes. If you go out and break the law or something everything is gonna fall on you, but good faith mistakes you learn from and go on. We don't criticize and we don't punish for good faith mistakes. As an example, two officers stopped to pass on some information, maybe personal business, and when they pulled away, one cut a turn too quickly and wiped out the side of both squad cars. I wrote them a note and said I could see where I could do the same thing myself. They (the cars) are in the shop being repaired, press on, don't worry about it. Because they didn't plan to do that, they will make sure for the rest of their natural lives they'll never do that again...why should anybody harp on the issue. It's not productive. Just put it behind you and get on. They feel more of a part of the organization...exactly that the car is a piece of equipment and they as people are more important. You don't have to beat them up and say be sure and don't damage squad cars, they know.

The emphasis on the people behind the role is evident in the comments of another (SF) chief of a large metropolitan police agency:

As far as a management philosophy, until somebody proves that they aren't to be trusted, I trust people. This thing is...the days of autocratic rule are gone...the idea that officers require extremely close supervision because they might do something wrong is childish. Unfortunately that does happen, but for the most part I think there should be an expectation that the people are dedicated enough...to go out and do it without being told...we all wear the same uniform, we've all got the same goals, we might have a different approach to these goals, but nevertheless we do have the same goals. My weakness is because I'm accessible, maybe too accessible to people... (I've been told) your gonna get some hard lumps as a result of that. I think that because I try to be tolerant, I think I'm more than kind.

Because of the Feeling Judgement process orientation toward people and their concerns, we might expect that SF's could get along well with other officers seeming to have the same orientation as they do in their work, police related or otherwise. This appears to be the case, especially when SF's recognized that associates who appeared to have the same philosophy as they were also NF's or SF's according to Myers-Briggs cognitive styles.

In a lot of ways, we have some real differences of opinion too (speaking about an NF associate). But then again when he does something, in my own mind I know why he's doing it...I wanna give him a bad time about being too easy, even though I know I would probably do the same thing. (Speaking about a different SF manager and associate) Oh, I can understand, sometimes I don't agree, but I understand I might have made the same decision because I probably relate too well to where he's coming from.

Similarly, an SF sergeant from a rural police department commented about his associations with a fellow officer sharing the same cognitive style.

John and I always have, ya know... John's on a different shift, but we've always been able to communicate well together and I guess when there are certain department situations that come up, we always seem to look at them in the same way...we always seem to have the same perspective.

The NT and Management Style:

NT's are usually referred to as being the standard executive type. Because the Thinking Judgement function is, by its very nature, a critical function, NT's are generally impersonal and objective, in addition to being matter-of-fact . They are interested in the broad picture and not in the necessary details of the job. This appearance of impersonality is also true with the ST's, the dominant group in law enforcement. Both of these styles share the same Judgement function, that of "Thinking" or making decisions with objective considerations rather than subjective ones (Feeling).

When the decision-making function in Jungian theory is discussed in seminars, many NT's and ST's make the comment "Hey, I have feelings too." Obviously we all have feelings, but we are not talking about the lack of having feelings, but the way we process information. Usually those who make decisions through the "Thinking" Judgement function lack the appearance of using the "Feeling" function as they comment and speak about things very objectively and pragmatically. As an example, read the following quote from an NT of a large department.

"I don't like the paperwork. I delegate most of that to my lieutenant. Pretty much it's been pure delegation. One of the things I haven't done is I haven't had a formal staff meeting...I don't wanna waste my time or their time having a staff meeting to say, hi, how are ya. If something comes to my attention I'll fire it to one of my lieutenants or sergeants and say I expect you to take care of this...I delegate it out and expect it to be done, so I don't do a lot of follow up unless...it wasn't done."

Another NT from a rural department with ten officers commented about the reason he likes his position:

Autonomy. I like to be in charge. I like to be able to make a difference. I like to be able to see things that need a change and make that change. I need to keep the ideas going and the challenge is much more than coming here day after day.

Note how the previous executive commented about change, which is the NT's strong suit because of the preference for variety, but never mentioned people or his desire to deal with them. Typically as this illustrates, the NT prefers to deal with tasks and make decisions with a very pragmatic logic.

ST's and Management Style:

The ST's, like the NT's, seem to describe their strengths in management as related to task management. They did, however, mention people more frequently in describing management style than when describing duties. This makes sense in that their primary job duties, at the time of the interviews, concern dealing with people. Still, as demonstrated by the following deputy chief's description of his organization, ST's tend to emphasize roles rather than the people filling them.

The people below me still have a direct connection to me and they are my ultimate employees or I'm the ultimate boss. We all...the four captains particularly all have interactions with the deputy chiefs...one controls the money and the transfers...another one has influence on investigations and discipline, and we run a rather open shop here so that they can interact with others.

Another ST deputy chief, after a reorganization of duties, was relived that he didn't have to deal with a lot of people problems anymore. *"I can do the others (people tasks)...but it's not much fun for me. Responsibility for a lot of other people's actions, ya know, that just wasn't much fun."*

He then went on to describe how he had reorganized:

"I was responsible for my own actions, didn't have a lot of subordinates to worry about. I put together a set of goals and objectives and I told the captains to write me a plan." You will notice in this discussion, that this ST

manager preferred to deal with task and not necessarily with people.

A ST deputy chief in charge of administration spoke about his managerial style as tough and forthright.

Well, I never though of myself as being particularly tactful or diplomatic, but these are some of the things I would hear from my subordinates...he's fair, but hard, he doesn't take any crap and he can see through shallow excuses. You know, if I tell somebody to do it, goddamn it I expect it to be done. Period! I've gotten better at that too. The part I disliked most was dealing with the personnel issues...I have pretty good organizational ability...in budget, planning and training.

Suggesting that perhaps his present duties involved more use of *"diplomacy than they were worth"*, this deputy chief remarked that he would go back out on the street "in a heartbeat" if his pay and benefits remained the same. He stated he often goes out on the street..he calls it *"a little R and R."* When he goes out to pull a shift, he said, *"I go out to arrest drunks and throw 'em in jail. That's exactly what I do."*

As the previous interviews and discussions indicate, the Feeling types, SF's and NF's, are generally people-oriented, while the NT's and the ST's are task-oriented. This seems to be the case whether they are on the street or in a management position.

CHAPTER 8

THE FEELING TYPES AND HOW THEY DIFFER

One would assume that being an NF in an ST world would be difficult and, in most cases, this was very true. Bearing in mind that Feeling types are in the minority in this occupation, one would expect they would feel a little out of place or different. This was certainly the case with the individuals I interviewed:

As I indicated before, several officers referred to themselves humorously as "oddballs". One Feeling type referred to himself as a "cigar store Indian standing in their (the department's) nice dining hall".

Despite their "oddness" relative to those with which they work, the NF managers all seem well adjusted. One reason for their lack of discomfort may be their relatively long tenure (18.9 years) and the ranks they hold. One would assume that many of the NF's who weren't comfortable left the police profession years ago feeling they didn't fit in.

A 6 foot 3 inch, 240 pound lieutenant with a rural sheriff's office commented that his size probably shielded him from potential aggravations and teasing from other officers:

Ya know I never thought about it, but it probably has come to my aid more than I'm willing to recognize. They think well, he might talk soft but he looks like he's able to back it up. Even when me and a partner would go to domestics we'd separate the couple and then my partner would want to leave. I was the one that would want to spend a little extra time ya know...just sitting down and trying to reason with them...find out what the deal was and help them out a little bit. My partner would say "ah come on and let's get some coffee, we'll be back here again later tonight when they go at it again". If I wanted to spend a little extra time, I did, and I really didn't get any guff from my partner about being too soft and..come to think of it, not from any other cop either.

Still, being a Feeling type caused some personal pain.

I would say, if anything, I was more caring, a lot more concerned. I think it caused me more emotional problems for myself because things would get to me. Pain bothered me more, I thought, than the average cop. I would let other people's pain bother me too much. I had an experience back when I was working patrol. I was on for three or four years. I had a double fatal chase. After that I almost quit. I always, I guess, from what other people said, had a lot more patience than other officers did. I could sit and listen more. In fact to this day even the dispatchers always say...one of them the other day said that I'm always even-keeled and very seldom can you see me get very excited and you seldom see me fly off the handle.

I can remember one night some years ago we wrestled some guy out of his house during a domestic...took him to the hospital for his drinking. He wasn't very happy. I went by the hospital to see him several days later. He couldn't believe that I would do that...and he wasn't somebody I knew either.

Another NF deputy sheriff shift supervisor knew he was different than the usual police officers.

Being different didn't bother me as much as it seemed to bother other people. So they must be the ones that have a problem with where I stand. I don't have any particular problem with where they stand, I don't wanna stand there, but I'm not going to deny them the right to stand there...so when the new hires come on and ask what the hell's this guy all about, they say, don't worry about him, he isn't gonna bother ya. ...hey, we have this cigar store Indian in our nice dining hall, but other than that, we still have a nice dining hall, he's a nice Indian, but he's still here.

This same officer, who holds an M.A. in Psychology, commented that the demographics of the department were changing. In order to be hired, an officer used to have to be from the local area. Additionally, in the early days, veteran's preference helped with getting a job in civil service. Now, however, that is not necessarily the case. The department is made up of individuals from all over the state now, and has grown to over 125 people. Many new officers coming on now don't have a military background.

This supervisor feels that as the pool of more experienced employees grows larger, his deviation from "true north" becomes less noticeable. He believes that the more diverse a police officer's background, the more accepting officers are with other employees being different than they are.

Another NF captain really enjoyed working the road (accidents and all), but he did not enjoy arresting people.

I did learn early in my career that I didn't like to arrest people. I always enjoyed driving fast...it makes the blood run, but I always felt bad in the routine traffic arrests. I wish I could give all those people a warning. The whole time I worked the road I never got over the fact I didn't like arresting people., I've worked the metro, specialized in training, taught defensive tactics, first aid, night stick use from range officers to whatever...and I still don't like arresting people.

Another NF captain, who holds a degree in education from a Lutheran denomination church college and who stands 6 foot 2 inches tall (230 pounds), commented about his differences from most other police officers:

Yes, I was different and it bothered me if somebody made a comment about "how the hell can you be in this job being so soft. I would have punched that guy long before that." (I was talking and negotiating with a violator long after they would have taken some physical action). Or they would be surprised if I got into a scuffle with someone because they felt that I usually would rather talk than fight. I've been in a shooting incident which came out ok. I ended up lifting weights with the guy who was later convicted of murder. I'm sure that didn't endear me to other officers in my station.

An NF street sergeant with a large suburban law enforcement agency spoke about his different approach to dealing with problems:

A lot of times I would come to the same conclusion as to what course of action to take in a given situation, but I think I took greater pains to smooth a situation over a little bit. When you had to tell a citizen or somebody that was really an arrested person...sometimes it tended to become a personal thing between an officer and a suspect or something...like you offended me so you are going to jail. I have always had a fairly aggressive enforcement stance...I don't apologize for people going to jail or arresting someone, but I have always made a strong effort to keep people satisfied. I want them to know that I'm not judging them personally, but judging what they have done and that's why they are in the position they are in. I've probably spent more time, maybe more time than I should have sometimes, hanging around to talk to people and tell them what we did or didn't do.

SF's recognize they are somewhat different than most of the other police officers in the way they deal with people. As an example, this officer (SF) stated:

I tended to pick partners that were similar to myself. Ya know oftentimes we handled, ya know, we always worked as a pair, and I wouldn't of picked a partner that would go blasting right in a place and start punching people out, I mean that is not my style.

He interestingly said he felt he was the exception when he first started police work twenty years ago (late 1960's), but felt that he would not necessarily be the exception now. He felt the concern for people and basic rights and dignity was more important than it was many years ago.

"I think law enforcement is changing. I think the make-up of the police department was quite different. More females, more diversified work force...higher education level..."

Recall that the NF sheriff's deputy who called himself a "cigar store Indian" said the same thing regarding the changing make-up of the police department.

The deputy chief (SF) of a large metropolitan agency commented that he was highly enforcement-oriented with *"... the highest misdemeanor arrest rating in the station for the four years I was on a power shift."* He characterizes himself as *"highly enforcement oriented, but by the same token, wanted to deal with satisfied customers."*

You can arrest the husband and father for domestic abuse or whatever it happens to be, but you are still dealing with the wife and you're still dealing with the kids and you are leaving the image of the department there. And I was always sensitive to that...I worked with some older guys that didn't necessarily have a high regard for enforcement...carried candy and stuff to give to kids on domestics and I was always touched by that kind of involvement. You are serving those folks and you've got to be selling yourself...always.

Another captain (SF) of a large metro agency characterize himself as being different from the other officers in his department. At rookie school he was quiet and reserved. *"I didn't fit into the military academy thing at all. I had to get out on my own. I didn't like that regimentation."* During the first part of the interview when asked if he felt others perceived him as being "soft" he said: *"No, I can be pretty miserable if I have to be. I don't like to, but I can. I used to have a real quick temper."*

Another SF sergeant, stationed in a rural sheriff's office, commented that he didn't think much about being different from other officers for the first part of his career because he worked alone most of the time. When he thought about the question he commented: *"Ah...with probably the majority of law enforcement officers, I've been told that I carry my feeling out on my sleeve too much."*

A rather outspoken SF lieutenant from a large metropolitan agency characterized "feeling differently" than most other officers: *"I'm much more friendly with people than most cops. I enjoy people. I like dealing with people. I like talking with people."*

ST's and NT's on being different:

Administrators who are NT's and ST's and decide things using pure objective criteria, are in the majority of how most police officers act, which is obvious since they constitute the largest group of cognitive styles in the profession. They do recognize, however, and know that the Feeling types, the NF's and SF's in their departments were different from themselves and the average police officer.

The reason ST's and NT's seem to get along well with each other is that both share the same method of making decisions-that of pure objectivity (Thinking). They do, however, have a difference in Perception. The reason this difference in Perception is not so obvious is because Perception is the taking in of information prior to making a decision. This taking in of information is usually non-verbal. The difference of Sensing and Intuition can be recognized through action, though. As an example of this difference, typically NT's are more global and future-oriented, looking down the road and not necessarily as grounded in detail as the ST's. Hence, they are usually not as good at remembering detail in the present sense.

The following deputy chief, an NT, commented:

We were riding through the district and there was a call about a robbery of a convenience store that had just taken place. I was driving and my partner said "come on we gotta go to this convenience store". I said to him "we're not going to catch him by going up there he's long gone from there". I said "let's drive by the other convenience store in our district and maybe we'll get lucky"...we drove up a side street, turned the head-lights off and drove down to the cross street and as we got to the intersection, the guy came running out with a shotgun...we bailed out of the car and chased him and caught the prick." It turned out there was a car up the street a ways where there was another guy, the lookout, with a driver. It seemed they had done three other very vicious stick-ups. If Bob had been driving we would have gone to the convenience store that was robbed because that's what you do.

This is an example of global thinking, or thinking ahead, not necessarily remaining tied to the detail of the moment. The NT captain commented that he had never been very good with remembering names, license plates, or detail. He had never found any stolen cars. For example, the only way he would know if a car was stolen was "if it ran into me on the street." He knows he is different from the other commanders around the city. Each morning when the other captains report to duty, they go through all of the incident reports from the night before to see what went on in their district. This chief, when he was a captain, assumed if something important occurred during the night watch he would be told about it.

Paying attention to detail or not being generally good at detail can be the primary difference between ST's and NT's. The reason, however, NT's and ST's don't usually see the difference is that one cannot necessarily see how a person is taking in information. A determination can only be made when a decision is made about the matter, either through telling what it means (Thinking) or telling what its value is (Feeling). The Judgement function is therefore a readily observable one. ST's, the predominant function in law enforcement, share the same Judgement function as the NT's. Hence, they may not easily recognize if they feel differently from one another.

Another example of paying attention to detail was demonstrated in a detective bureau where one ST and one NT were teamed up in a crime scene search group. The NT would do a crime scene search, finding evidence, mapping locations, bagging up evidence, and other detail work, and invariably, the ST would come along and find additional evidence missed by the NT. The NT's preferred method of Perception caused him to skim over the scene and miss important detail.

What Happens to Most of Those Who Feel Different:

An interesting implication surfaces here. If someone comes into the police profession, or any profession for that matter, and finds they feel "out of place", they would obviously have a tendency to leave and find some other employment.

Several colleagues and I conducted a study at a technical college in Minnesota regarding those individuals who were part of a police training class. In Minnesota, if you want to become a law enforcement officer, you must first attend a two year program at a technical college, university or community college and then take a "skills course" for an eight week period of time. This then enables you to be licensed. The new students in the law enforcement class were given the Myers-Briggs along with a series of other assessment instruments and tests. To avoid self- fulfilling prophecies, the results of the Myers Briggs instrument were not disclosed to the students. They were told that if they wanted to see the results of this one instrument, they could come to the counseling office and the results would be explained to them. We did this to ensure that students who were of an uncommon cognitive type in law enforcement did not see their results and decide that the profession was not the best for them on that parameter alone. We felt that, even though their scores may reflect cognitive styles not commonly found in law enforcement, uncommon types bring special strengths to the profession. Only one student asked to see the results of the instrument. The distribution of the cognitive Judgement styles of this class was 80% Thinking and 20% Feeling, the same general Myers-Briggs description of a group of veteran police officers with twenty years on the job.

The results of this distribution would lead one to believe that rookie cops do not necessarily become socialized into being less compassionate cops after being on the job for a period of time. It would appear the occupation's tasks attract those whose strengths are matter-of-fact, practical, logical, direct and rational, fair, structured and just, in a logical sort of way. This would seem to explain why cops, who generally appear to be cold, condescending, serious acting, and authoritarian could appear to be that way as a result of preferences which Jung felt were constitutional, or present at birth or shortly thereafter. This is generally contrary to some sociologists theories of the 1960's and 1970's, these theories being that police working personalities, or "why cops act like cops", were the direct result of the influence of veteran cops on rookie cops. Many sociologists feel that if law enforcement agencies specifically recruited warm, feeling, and compassionate individuals, the police services would become more warm and compassionate. The above results seem to indicate that warm, nurturing, compassionate individuals would not necessarily be attracted to the profession anyway, due to the nature of the task required in performing in the profession.

Size May Affect Success:

It was interesting to note that one-half of the Feeling types of the classes studied left before their two year graduation. Most of them cited "incompatibility" with the program. This would seem to reinforce the issue that people are attracted to jobs in which they can use their strengths. As a cross check, we administered the instrument to two more successive classes, and in the next several years, the distribution remained the same as that of veteran police forces.

This brings up additional interesting issues. All but one of the NF's interviewed was at least six feet tall and all weighed at least 200 pounds. The one that was 5 foot 10 and one-half inches, lifted weights and was noticeably muscular. The law enforcement profession is primarily masculine, characterized by the rough and tumble, physical situations that the media portrays. Fighting, chases, shootings, struggles, and macho images are portrayed continually. I would say that, because of the large, imposing physical size of these officers, their "deviations from true north", by displaying compassion, was not challenged as it may have been had they have been smaller in stature.

For example, if a police officer were a smaller male with a Judgement preference for Feeling, he may have been intimidated by other officers through kidding, cajoling, or teasing. As those officers began to realize that they seemed different from other police officers, they may have decided the law enforcement profession wasn't for them. I do not believe this to be necessarily true in the case of women police officers who are typically smaller in stature than their male counterparts. In fact, precisely because they are women, male officers might expect compassion as a cultural norm for them and leave them alone.

Being a Feeling type in law enforcement as well as a minority may be a self-fulfilling prophesy as far as job tenure is concerned. Many Feeling types may tend to be uncomfortable and may leave for another occupation, which means there are more Thinking types represented. But the critical issue is, as you can see from the interviews, those few remaining Feeling types who desire to remain for whatever reason, give the occupation an interesting depth.

The reverse is probably true for the helping professions, such as social workers and corrections personnel. There the majority of decisions are made through social value and the majority of the people in these occupations are Feeling types. A person with an objective, basic, practical, matter-of-fact, judgement function, may feel uncomfortable with a group of people expressing individual compassion, human concern, and are gentle, sensitive and caring. Both, naturally, would want to associate with groups of individuals more like themselves.

Police administrators, sociologists, and others need to recognize that the tasks involved in the policing profession are those that appeal to the Thinking types. Those are structured, sometimes cold, generally impersonal, logical, objective, and matter-of-fact. Sociologists' desire to have a warm, nurturing, caring, feeling police agencies that demonstrate a lot of compassion may be impossible to a large extent. We may and really should teach officers to be more people-oriented, but because of the nature of the job tasks and the natural attraction to the Thinking types, officers will probably not be that way naturally.

CHAPTER 9

POSSIBLE WEAKNESSES OF EACH STYLE

All of the different styles bring certain strengths to the profession. Obviously people may tend to display some of the weaknesses of those various styles.

An understanding of Myers-Briggs brings a new dimension into how people function on the job and the effect that weaknesses in taking in information and making decisions can have on their performance.

Potential Weaknesses of Intuitive Feelers:

Despite strengths, NF's also reported some weaknesses that differentiate them from ST's. Some of the potential areas in need of development by those preferring the NF functions are listed by Hirsh and Kummerow as:

1.   May not be seen as sufficiently tough-minded;

2.   May try to please too many people at the same time;

3.   May need to pay more attention to the details of the task as to the concerns of people.

One NF, the chief of a large agency, recognized his being different from others as being politically vulnerable. He had been told by others that he was too humane. *"You're going to get hurt. You're letting your feelings interfere with your operation,"* was how they put it.

Another NF operating as a chief of a large metropolitan agency was aware of MBTI typology. He purposefully appointed an individual that he knew was good at detail (a ST) to *"handle the details."* He spoke of conceptualizing what needed to be done and then asking his assistant to fill in the blanks and make it work. He knew he strengths were not in handling the details and that he would not do as good a job as the ST. As a result of their teaming together and using both strengths, the tasks were handled well.

Two of the individuals in the NF group had difficulties switching from the street to management because of their concern for the feelings and friendship of others. Simply put, their concern for people got in the way of their managerial roles.

One NF characterized it as follows:

When I became a supervisor, I guess I didn't know how to handle that. I felt that staying in that character of being one of the guys didn't work out because a lot of the guys didn't respect that, they didn't work for me, they didn't do their job, they thought that what the hell, this guy is...well you know, so I came on a bit too strong and too severe and that wasn't supported by the department so I've been spending the last few years backing way off and trying to be more understanding...I tend now to be a little too nice.

He commented that he feels more comfortable now in being a *"bit more friendly,and warmer. Sometimes you lose who the hell you are in trying to be someone that you are not".*

As an example of the above comment, some Feeling types may have a tendency to become "hard-assed" as supervisors. This can be explained by looking at type dynamics as follows:

An NF personality type would indicate Intuition or Feeling being dominant functions, with Thinking and Sensing as either tertiary or the inferior function. Individuals often have difficulty being someone that they are not. According to type dynamics, individuals in an organization whose tasks are primarily Sensing and Thinking, such as law enforcement, but whose strong preferences are social value (Feeling), may try to emulate ST traits and overcompensate resulting in more of a strict personal interpretation of how to act.

They may become very autocratic and hard in an attempt to act as those around them, and deny their feelings and concerns for people as inappropriate for those in the police occupation.

In two instances, when I explained they Myers-Briggs instrument to police managers, tears formed in the eyes of individuals who showed NF preferences. Both had characterized themselves as real "hatchet men" at work. They said they had pushed their concern for people aside, believing that concern didn't belong in management, particularly in management of a paramilitary organization such as a law enforcement agency.

Type theory assumes that people are born with a predisposition to prefer some functions over others. For example, a person who develops Sensing in a highly differentiated way is likely to become an astute observer of the immediate environment. While attention is directed to the specifics of the environment, the person spends less time using the opposite function, in this case, Intuition. Myers and McCaulley (1985) state that environment becomes extremely important since environmental factors can foster development of preferences or discourage their natural bent by reinforcing activities that are less satisfying. This can result in less skillful use of natural strengths. Based on my studies, it seems clear that some individuals in law enforcement, who prefer the Feeling function, may overcompensate while trying to balance the use of pure logic (Thinking) with social value (Feeling) and become dictatorial and autocratic.

Indeed, this type-related dilemma seems tailor-made for an occupation like law enforcement. Generally speaking, law enforcement attracts primarily ST's. This being the case, when NF's become cops, they either have to try to fit in by "copying" others and their actions, or just accept their differences and try to adjust. Many cannot adjust so they leave, stating they "just didn't fit in". Others, when they try to act in areas which are not their strengths, may become frustrated and really not "true to themselves."

Jung felt that such attempts could not work in the long term. He wrote that trying to be what you are not usually results in neurosis and/or generalized exhaustion over a long period of time.

I should note that the potential imbalance, which the presence of uncommon types can foster, need not be unilateral. If an ST was to find himself "trapped" in a warm, nurturing, unstructured environment, such as that created by a NF supervisor, he might be extremely uncomfortable. This type of environment would typically be characterized by lots of smiling, chatting, hugs and pats on the back, and lots of overt concern for the employee's welfare. For these types, a structured, realistic, practical, systematic, and concrete task-oriented organization would be much preferable because of its consistent and systematic rules.

An excellent example of imbalance, or "trying to act in a different way than is natural," was noted in the comments of an NF commander assigned to a southern precinct. He had a reputation of being strict, "too strict by today's standards." To him it was "my way or no way." His primary concerns were how the officers felt about him and if they still liked him rather than if they were doing the right job in the field.

To tell you, I damn near quit in the first two or three months. I decided this stuff wasn't for me (supervision). I felt like a fish out of water. I felt uncomfortable supervising guys that had three times the time I had on the force. I had some times that I went nose to nose with some guys and I hadn't backed down and I stumbled a few times. I had my boss tell me to lighten up a little bit. Some of the guys perceived me as maybe a pushover. I took a survey a couple times a year on how I was doing...one thing that used to come up pretty frequently was the hard line I took on (my) people.

This commander acknowledged that being a supervisor has been hard on him. As a result, even though he had chances for several additional promotions, he turned them all down. He is looking forward to retiring and doing something other than law enforcement.

Potential Weaknesses of Sensing-Feelers:

While the Sensing-Feeling function gravitates around Feeling-derived Judgments, SF's possess a strong reliance on Sensing. This grounds them in concrete issues and interactions. Hirsh and Kummerow list several possible pitfalls for SF's. They may:

1.   Not be seen as being sufficiently tough-minded (the same problem as NF's);

2.   Need to consider global issues as well as present considerations;

3.   May attempt to avoid conflict.

As I mentioned before, one SF commented about being too soft, and recognized this characteristic as making him politically vulnerable. The other police manager had said, *"You're too humane, you're gonna get hurt. You are letting your feelings interfere with your operation."*

There appears to be a pronounced job focus among the SF's, as is usually the case with the mainstream ST's. They typically do not report many outside interests other than those around law enforcement. Even within the field itself, they exhibit fewer dramatic role changes than others, particularly the NT's. Apparently the SF's seek to do their jobs well, but do not often look for lateral or upward transfers. They, for the most part, seem to be tied up in performing their jobs in an excellent manner.

The Potential Weaknesses of the "True Norths", the ST's and the NT's:

The activities of a beat cop seem perfectly suited to the inclinations of an ST. They feature rapid, unpredictable chains of events in which maintaining one's "cool" is essential. However, Kummerow and Hirsh listed the following possible weaknesses that may affect some individuals preferring the ST function:

1.   May neglect important personal issues;

2.   May overlook long-range implications for day-to-day activities;

3.   May appear blunt and insensitive.

Of the group of ST managers interviewed, several cemented on the fact that they didn't like to deal with personnel problems. One was relieved when a personnel function was re-assigned from him to someone else. None felt they were different from the majority of other police officers, and some even pointedly asked if they should feel differently from other police officers.

Based on this information, it seems clear that ST's like and feel comfortable within the police culture's emphasis on impersonal, logical interaction. They seem to sense they fit in and may even yearn for the opportunity to return to this style of behavior if placed in other positions which require a more personal, warm and human approach.

As the words of the NF who described himself as a *"deviation from true north"*, the ST's personify the *"tough cop"*. They are what most people, in and out of the profession, refer to as the *"true north"* barometers of how cops usually conduct themselves.

As with the other functions, Hirsh and Kummerow also list potential pitfalls for those preferring the NT function:

1.   An NT may be too impersonal and unappreciative of others input;

1.   Forgetful of current realities;

2.   Unable or unwilling to focus on practical details.

None of the NT's commented on being too tough or not appreciating people enough. This makes sense as they make decisions with pure logic as the ST's do, and generally would not even consider they may not appreciate people. While many NT's in law enforcement act impersonally, they may not believe that they do. They probably do not have the insight to see whether they do or not. This seems particularly likely in the context of their work in the realistic, impersonal, and logical world of law enforcement. Several commented on their lack of attention to detail. One NT stated that he was never any good at remembering names, license plates or details of a homicide. Another commented about his partner *"driving him crazy with constant detail."*

As an example of inattention to detail, during one incident, an NT manager of a police academy called a meeting with five ST subordinates for twelve o'clock noon to discuss various instructional issues. As the meeting progressed, the ST's became irritated at the length of the meeting. The NT manager explained that he had told them the length of the meeting in the memo he had sent them. The ST's protested that he had not, nor had he mentioned that they should cancel their other classes, nor where the meeting was to be held. The NT supervisor retrieved the memorandum he had sent, and after re-reading it, realized that he had neglected to mention not only the expected length of the meeting, but also the subject matter and where the meeting was to be held. He later mentioned that he had apparently "just assumed" he had furnished all of the details to the others.

CHAPTER 10

CONFLICTS WITH OTHER PROFESSIONS

Since the advent of cops, "newsies", social workers and "shrinks," there have been misunderstandings and conflicts in communications and in understanding the motives and methodology in how each does their job. Police ask that details be withheld from a story and then see them in print, or police officers withhold information in a high profile case that the media needs. This is certainly not the case with every reporter who ever came around a police precinct, or with every social worker who dealt with juvenile divisions, but generally there has been misunderstanding and conflicts with those professions more than others.

This conflict has been chalked off to describing each other in less than the glowing terms of "jack booted Nazi cops" to "bleeding heart liberals" as the professions look at each other in somewhat less than understanding ways. We may have considered that the objectives of each job were different for each occupation. A person would think, though, that even if the jobs were different, they all deal in the criminal justice field. So what could be the difference that makes people in these occupations look at issues in a way different than law enforcement?

A look at these various occupations through the use of the Myers-Briggs Cognitive Styles reflects some interesting reasons which can help explain why these inherent differences exist. We already know that the predominate cognitive style in the police profession is Sensing-Thinking (ST), with the least represented style as Intuitive-Feeling (NF). An interesting fact to note is that the CAPT data bank reflects a sample of editors and reporters, along with a sample of social workers, as having predominant cognitive styles of Intuitive-Feeling (NF), which is the least represented in law enforcement. No wonder both occupations look at things differently.

Editors and Reporters:

Table 10. Editors and Reporters According to MBTI Cognitive Styles. N = 113

		Percent	Number
Intuitive-Feeling	NF	41.71	46
Sensing-Feeling	SF	16.82	19
Intuitive-Thinking	NT	27.43	31
Sensing-Thinking	ST	15.04	17
Totals		100.00	113

*Data Source: Macdaid, Gerald P., Mary H. McCaulley et al, (1986)

91

The majority of this sample of editors and reporters is 42 percent Intuitive-Feeling, while in the police sample, the Intuitive-Feeling types were only 6.3 percent. With this vast difference in the way people are looking at issues, no wonder there is somewhat of a rub in relationships and a lack of understanding between the two professions.

Look at this scenario: A police investigator picks up the morning newspaper and reads about a case he has worked on the day before, and often times doesn't even recognize it. There are several reasons for this. One may be that he couldn't give the information to the reporter, or was unable to get a copy of the report to the reporter. Here lies the rub. The reporter, being global in perspective (Intuitive) generally gets the facts in the main ballpark which, in his or her perception , is "close enough", while the cop, who knows the intimate details of the case, sees broad generalities and error in the story.

Bearing in mind, the police officer, being typically Sensing (perceiving in great detail) has a hard time understanding, from his point of view, why the reporter didn't say "at precisely 10:32 am, the victim descended the stairs and was accosted by the perpetrator, who inserted a seven inch blade of a filet knife through the victims outer clothing into a space between the sixth and seventh rib on the right side of the victim's rib cage." This only concerns the perceptive part of the issue. Now, realize that the Judgement side of the coin, the decision making part of cognition also is looked at from two completely different sides of the issue.

The reporter, deciding with the preferred use of the Feeling function, will look at the case with social value

(Feeling), considering both the fate of the victim, but also considering the human side of the crook, the family, the spouse, friends, and neighbors. While the police investigator is still trying to wash the blood off of his or her hands after the crime scene, the reporter is writing about the poor assailant who was raised in a broken home by an alcoholic single parent who is really sorry that the child got into trouble, but really didn't commit this crime and, the police must have beaten a confession out of the assailant anyway. Of course, the story the reporter is writing is a legitimate human interest story that readers are interested in. The police officer is looking at the issue through the pragmatic, objective lens (Thinking), and logically thinks the crook should be on his way to the gallows, not out on the street on bail.

Obviously this may be somewhat of an exaggeration, but it brings home the fact that the way people generally look at things can result in real differences in how people view the world.

Social Workers:

The same differences hold true for social workers, another occupational group which often sees itself on opposite sides of an issue from the police. Since we all may look at an issue through a different lens, we have a tendency to see things from our own perspective. We are obviously not making a judgement on who may be "right or wrong" on an issue, but merely stating that our perspectives could be somewhat different.

Table 11. Social Workers According to MBTI
Cognitive Styles. N = 479

		Percent	Number
Intuitive-Feeling	NF	42.59	204
Sensing-Feeling	SF	21.50	103
Intuitive-Thinking	NT	18.58	89
Sensing-Thinking	ST	17.33	83
Totals		100.00	479

*Data Source: Macdaid, Gerald P, Mary H. McCaulley et al, (1986)

The Feeling Judgement function in this group is over 64 percent. This means that a great majority of social workers prefer making decisions considering social value rather than pure logic. Taking the tasks of their occupation into consideration this conclusion would appear appropriate.

During my law enforcement career, I served some time in a narcotics enforcement section during the early 1970's, as I am sure many of you have. One of the duties was training various other governmental agencies on drug identification, drug laws, and investigations. I can't count the numerous times I was treated like an "undesirable" by some social workers when I lectured to local and state representatives of social service departments. Many seemed to just wait stoically until the question and answer period began and then gleefully asked if I enjoyed putting poor little teenagers who were "just smoking a little weed" into jail. They seemed to love discussing the philosophy of punishment and incarceration versus treatment. Surely I was as uncomfortable around this group of individuals who, to me seemed not to really understand the importance strict law enforcement played in the problems of the drug culture, as I'm sure they were with me as a law enforcement representative.

Prior to leaving my career with the department of public safety, I had recent occasion to work with the social service department regarding a preliminary study geared to improve the state's computer systems dealing with battered women and domestic violence. As I talked with several social department administrators, we discussed the operations of civil divisions in sheriff's departments. One of the managers made an unsolicited statement about how he disliked "police types". His partner, who was listening to the conversation over the office divider, chimed in with several additional comments along the same general line. I chuckled to myself as I listened to their comments about police insensitivity, they of course not realizing they were talking with a law enforcement administrator and not a computer researcher. This seemed to reinforce the issue of the observable differences we have between occupations.

Why the Conflict:

People usually feel most comfortable with those we understand, can communicate well with, and whose values we seem to share. When we find ourselves in a situation where that is not the case, we have a tendency to feel uncomfortable. The others don't seem to understand our point of view. Those of us in law enforcement may feel people in the helping occupations are unrealistic, fuzzy headed, and too liberal. Even though a person is deemed innocent until proven guilty, we in law enforcement know when we arrest them they are usually guilty, right? We know the world is full of unprincipled, lying, cheating, stealing low lifes. We also know the social workers, probation officers, defense bar, and the psychologists are trying to get these degenerates back out on the street faster than we can bring them in, right? The media's point of view may not make a lot of sense to us either, as we make our judgments through pure, objective, and logical reasoning. No wonder law enforcement personnel appear to be cold, hard hearted, non-compassionate human beings in the eyes of those who prefer to make their decisions through warm human insight and subjective reasoning.

The Myers-Briggs Type Inventory, based on Jungian Typology, gives us logical, rational reasons to understand why people look at issues the way they do. It also gives us a terminology which we can apply to the different personality types. We can then use this terminology as a tool to understand the different ways we all make decisions as well as the whys we make those decisions for totally different reasons and from totally different directions.

I look back on my career experiences with the helping professions and now understand why they seemed to look at issues in a completely different light than I. I truly believe that if all sides are aware of the differences in perception and judgement, we can better understand each other's points of view and work more as a team in the criminal justice area.

CHAPTER 11

WOMEN IN LAW ENFORCEMENT

As we have discussed, law enforcement is a structured, logical, matter-of-fact occupation. Women have just begun to enter the occupation in greater numbers throughout the country.

June Singer commented that Carl Jung believed psychological type, as defined by the differences in Perception and Judgement, may be present at birth as part of the "psychological constitution" of the <u>infant, not male or female child</u> (writer's emphasis). This is true at least in the sense of predispositions towards certain functions and attitudes, and the behaviors stemming from those attitudes. Jung was of the opinion that men comprised most of the Extraverted Thinking types. He asserted that a woman's Feeling function reflected the corresponding values of society and that value of Feeling was the result of the true desire of women who reflected those feelings.

However, Jung wrote his book on types in Switzerland in 1921 and echoed the values of that era. According to Singer, if Jung would have had an opportunity to observe the highly differentiated thinking of the women in the United States today, he may not have reached that conclusion.

A colleague and I had an opportunity to administer the Myers-Briggs Form G, self-scorable instrument to 82 female police officers who were part of a group of over 500 women attending the International Association of Women's Police Conference in St. Paul, Minnesota, in 1990.

Prior to taking the instrument, the women police officers were cautioned several times to be sure to answer the questions as they truly felt they <u>personally</u> preferred, not as they felt their occupation or specific organizations expected them to be.

Table 13: Women Police Officers at the International Association of Women Police Conference, St. Paul, Mn. September, 1990. N = 82

		Percent	Number
Intuitive-Feeling	NF	20.80	17
Sensing-Feeling	SF	24.40	20
Intuitive-Thinking	NT	17.00	14
Sensing-Thinking	ST	<u>37.80</u>	<u>31</u>
Totals		100.00	82

In table 13, it is interesting to note that the NF function in this group of female police officers somewhat resembles the general normative population sample expected in the population (20.8% to 28.32%). The SF preference is lower in this sample, 24.4 percent, to the normative sample of 29.34 percent. The NT function resembles the general population (17.0% to 17.56%), and the ST function is higher at 37.80% to 24.78%. The SF and ST preferences being high makes sense in that the occupation calls for those "S" Sensing strengths, but the 45.2 percent preferring the Feeling function in making decisions is vastly different than that of other police officer samples comprised primarily of men.

The police occupation generally reflects the ST preference with the NF preference being greatly under-represented - but here we have a group of police officers who tend to resemble the general population.

Women police administrators have been a part of my research, but because they have only begun to rise into the upper ranks, they represent only a small percentage of the total group of police executives in my study. With some departments, there was only one single female in the sworn ranks. The women's MBTI preferences reflected the general police population, ST's and NT's, but definitely a T in their Judgement preferences.

Isabel Myers stated that the working assumption of type theory is that each person has "true" preferences. There are some reasons why, when taking the instrument, that type preferences may be incorrectly reported. One of these reasons is that tension may exist regarding one's own preferences and those of people around them.

Taking into consideration that the vast majority of police officers are ST or NT; women in the police profession may tend to reflect those attitudes rather than their "true" type. Additionally, the questions may be answered in terms of one's perception of what behavior is expected and valued in an occupation.

In the case of police tasks and general attitude, compassion and personal social value is not necessarily appreciated, nor expected in the occupation. Isabel Myers said possible confusion in cultural attitudes is most likely to take place in the TF scale. Culturally, people often equate feeling, compassion, and warmth with feminine attributes, and cold, hard logic and rationality with masculinity. Clearly, the law enforcement profession's tasks reflect cold, hard reality.

The results of the instrument the women took while attending the conference raises a very interesting question. Being away from a work setting in a casual, relaxed conference setting may have produced more valid MBTI results, particularly after being coached several times to answer the questions in a personal way rather than an occupational way. Additionally, being in a supportive group of over five hundred women police officers for over five days and perhaps feeling more validated through sharing experiences common only to women, may possibly have contributed to more valid results.

Being in a predominately male occupation involves intensive peer pressure to "conform to the majority" in many instances of police work. Being in a group of women police at a conference may have reduced the result of peer pressure to act as the majority of male officers would act back in their own departments.

Another consideration of the results of the MBTI is the dynamics of why women in policing would want to have a police conference in the first place, and what is the nature of the women attending the conference. Because of the large percentage of Feeling types at the conference, did they attend because they are painfully aware of their differences on the job and want the opportunity to share it with others experiencing the same stresses?

There are several interesting issues to consider. In Minnesota, of the students entering higher educational institutions for the expressed intent of becoming a police officer, twenty-five percent are women. Of those graduating, only five percent are women. Women may see the occupation one way as they begin school and then see it in a much different light part way through, and, as a result, leave. Women may tend to bring more personal value and compassion to the field, but, when surrounded by a majority of ST's in the educational process, decide the occupation is not for them. If this is the case, it continues to confirm the theory that most people are attracted to occupations dealing with and addressing their strengths.

An interesting issue to consider may be, if the nature of the job of policing changes, would it appeal to more SF's and NF's hereby attracting more to the occupation? Would the occupation then begin to change because of more concern for human value, and continue to attract and retain more Feeling types because their comfort level would be growing as the majority of ST's and NT's diminishes. Would this occupation resemble the general population, as far as Jungian Typology and Myers-Briggs Cognitive Styles is concerned, if more women were to become a part of the occupation and stay?

During my presentation to this group at the National Association of Women Police Conference, I asked them what personality attributes, in their opinion, were important to the occupation of being a police officer. First on the list was the ability to communicate, second was the ability to make a quick, sound decision, and the third was the need for compassion.

These are interesting thoughts, particularly in this time of public complaint about the apparent lack of compassion in the field.

CHAPTER 12

BENEFITS OF MYERS-BRIGGS IN POLICING

The Myers-Briggs Type Indicator is an excellent tool to help explain behaviors in the workplace. Experience has shown me, along with reasons listed by Ronald Lynch and Hobie Henson, that there are several excellent uses of Jungian typology in the police profession:

1. As a team building tool. Those who take the instrument are able to recognize and accept differences in communication styles.

2. As an aid in looking at issues from different perspectives.

3. As an aid to officers in understanding why they may feel uncomfortable in certain job situations.

4. As a parameter during recruitment, not to screen out those types uncommon to law enforcement, but to help give applicants better tools to understand personal strengths and possible weaknesses. Additionally, it may help applicants

understand the general culture they are becoming a part of. **The Myers-Briggs should not be used to screen out applicants.** As you can see, there are very successful individuals of every type in all occupations.

I believe the Myers-Briggs Type Indicator should not be used alone to singularly predict the potential of an individual's ability to perform a specific job. An excellent rationale is to look at the results of studies reflected in this book. Persons of all cognitive styles can perform the job of policing. Typically, as we have discussed, the law enforcement's Myers-Briggs cognitive occupational preference is ST. One may assume all ST's would make good police officers. Obviously this is not the case. There are bright ST's and dull ST's, motivated and unmotivated ST's. My research shows that NF's, who comprise only .05% of the officers in the profession, add greatly to the quality of the occupation even though their strengths do not necessarily speak to the general tasks of the job. If the MBTI were used to screen those who didn't fit the ST profile, or were used to recommend to applicants they shouldn't seek a profession based on the instrument alone, we would lose out on the diversity that uncommon types bring to the occupation. As an example, an ST may bring refreshing structure and reality to a group of N's who are intuitively dealing with an issue, while an NF may bring a global and a compassionate perspective to a cold, stark, logical task being planned by a group of ST's.

In its use as a team building tool, it has been my experience to observe numerous instances where Jungian Typology proved to be an excellent tool for explaining change. As an example, the chief of a major metropolitan police agency was an NT. He had two assistants, an NT and an ST. The chief communicated very well with both assistants, but spoke more of change and general conceptual operational issues, such as re-organization, with the NT. Both administrators who shared the NT preferences would travel to various conferences and symposiums together. Because both communicated well together in global terms, they would discuss new technology and attempt to institute change within the organization with less than optimal success. When this issue was discussed during a team building session based on Myers-Briggs Cognitive Styles, it became evident that the persons who favored the NT preference were too global in their applications and re-organizational issues and were missing numerous details necessary for the successful implementation of any change. Because of their familiar communication patterns and ease of understanding each other, they were inadvertently excluding the administrator with the ST preference from the critical areas of discussion-that of the actual details necessary in implementing the changes. The NT administrators, including the administrator with the ST preference, the preference shared by the large majority of people charged with carrying out policy changes, agreed that the individual with the ST preference would serve as a "leavening agent" in the planning discussions to ensure a methodical, step-by -step process would be used in implementing changes within the department.

Another example of an administrator using the MBTI in the operational areas of a police organization deals with communication styles. A deputy chief, an NT, recognized the necessity of communicating in a more acceptable "tone" when issuing written directives to the sworn officers as a whole. Even though the majority of police officers are ST's, they still can be affected negatively by a "curt" writing style, typical of NT's or ST's. Recognizing the need to communicate in a more conciliatory tone, he would ask an individual he called, "one of his few token feelers," (an NF), to look over the memoranda and make any form changes he deemed appropriate. The NF would revise the memoranda slightly, not changing the content, but only the tone of the form, to give it a more "humane" touch.

I observed another, more pragmatic, approach after a team building session I had facilitated with a group of police managers. One individual, whose preference was ST, selected a planning committee by going over the MBTI grid which listed his staff. He picked competent individuals from each of the various functions to serve as members. He wanted input from as many points of view as possible. He wanted ST's, who bring facts and present realities; NT's, who bring a global, planning perspective to the table; and SF's and NF's, who bring values, personal subjective judgments and commitments.

Another strong benefit of the MBTI concerns understanding why some officers perform better at some tasks than others. As an example, one investigator had been in a detective bureau in a large suburban department for many years. He had been a uniform patrol officer and later, had risen through the ranks. He never was content or comfortable, however, in the occupation. Obviously he was able to perform the job is a satisfactory manner, but always seemed to be at loose ends; not "really fitting in" with the rest of the officers. They felt he was "kind of drifty" not sticking to the task at hand, and going off in a lot of different directions. He took the MBTI and found his preferred functions were NT, with his dominant being Intuition. After an explanation of the results of the instrument, he began to understand why he was uncomfortable around Sensing types, along with their lack of accepting him and his not quite fitting in. He was able to transfer into a job which was research-based, dealing with computers, intelligence data, and special projects, and became a strong contributor to the investigative process. He has since gone on to graduate school with the intentions of becoming a counseling psychologist.

Another example deals with much the same situation with a patrol officer in another large city. He had been on the road for several years, enjoyed being a cop, but was very uncomfortable with the confrontations with motorists and some other, less pleasant duties connected with traffic accidents. Even though he was talented in his ability to deal with people, he was thinking of leaving the occupation. He took the MBTI to try to get a handle on where his real interests were. What he found was that he preferred NF functions, the type that comprises only five percent of police officers. Understanding this, he sought and obtained a transfer into the photographic and media unit. There he performed in an outstanding manner.

The MBTI has been maligned occasionally by a few psychologists because it shows only positive aspects of how a person functions. This, to me, is a narrow view of what understanding the MBTI can do. Its purpose is not to serve as a predictor of behavior, but as one tool of many in the complex world of human psychology to help us understand ourselves and why we relate to our jobs the way we do. If it can help people understand how they each prefer to look at issues in their daily lives and to appreciate these differences, it has served us all well.

As you can see, the common types in law enforcement, the ST's and the NT's, the less common SF's, and the least common NF's can all perform the job of policing. All of the various types bring differing strengths to the occupation. The more we understand individuals and their various preferences and attitudes, the closer we can come to understanding the profession. It is obvious that the attitudes and behaviors of police officers are not simple phenomena. The MBTI gives us an excellent opportunity to observe the complex world of police behavior in a completely different light.

A WORD ABOUT LEADERSHIP

The information contained in this book should offer you some excellent insight into the people who perform the day to day activities involved in the operations of your department. As I mentioned before, it will also help you understand some of the reasons people in other occupations that we deal with on a daily basis look at issues in a different way than we in law enforcement do.

Now that you have taken the time to read through a different view into the complex world of personalities in law enforcement, I wanted to expand somewhat on issues dealing with leadership in the police profession today.

The word *"leadership"* has been thrown around for a number of years, with numerous definitions used and schools and seminars on leadership touted, all with mixed results. We really should measure the various books and articles which have been written about management, leadership and empowerment in the last several years by the metric ton, not by the volume. Most of us have attended many leadership classes in the past years and probably consider ourselves to be fairly effective leaders when, in fact, we may be less than we would believe ourselves to be. We need to look at some of the reasons why this may be true and what changes we can make to become more effective leaders.

An interesting employee phenomenon has been occurring in the work-place and will continue to grow into the next millennium. We are all starting to notice it. That is, employees are starting to ask a lot of questions about their jobs, why their organizations are run as they are, and why managers make the decisions they do. This is very true in all types of occupations, not only in the police profession. There are several reasons for this change, but the primary one is the increased knowledge-base of our young officers that are on the job today.

The Growth of Knowledge:

The profusion of radio stations, television channels, newspapers, books, and available educational opportunities, has caused the intellectual level of our employees to grow in leaps and bounds. General knowledge is increasing at an incredible rate. We need to realize that ninety percent of all scientists throughout the history of humankind, including physical and behavioral scientists, are living today. They are generating a lot of knowledge.

As we know, many law enforcement agencies require a minimum of two years of post secondary education for entry level jobs, with most requiring four year degrees for promotions. With this level of knowledge, its no wonder those officers in the entry to mid-level positions put pressure on less educated, more senior, officers in a rather structured civil service, merit system hierarchy. Obviously, this is the case not only in police organizations, but in private industry as well. It's important that police administrators recognize this dramatic increase in intellect and desire to learn. We all have extremely intelligent and talented employees. Many want a "piece of the action" so to speak. A lot of them would really like to "try your chair on for size", but few of them really have the ability to do just that (nor, once they tasted command, would want to put up with what you have to put up with). One effective way to deal with this paradigm shift is to realize that the days of "I tell and you do" management are fading fast.

Autocratic Management is a Thing of the Past:

Most of us moved up through the ranks from working the street. As we all know, the nature of policing on the street reinforces the necessity of making immediate, authoritative decisions. Most of the decisions we made on the street were made in a "crisis" mode. We gained confidence in making independent determinations of fact. We were praised and rewarded for operating with split-second timing. As we moved up the ladder, some of us viewed our autocratic supervisors of twenty years ago as role models. Why not? We didn't really have anyone else to model ourselves after as we moved up from sergeant to lieutenant, to captain, deputy chief, and then to chief or sheriff. Most of us, if we are truthful, will admit we still have a tendency to overuse independent decision making when faced with day-to-day problems. We really need to learn to slow down and take the time to gather additional information prior to making decisions.

Share the Power:

There are problems which require immediate answers in the field, but rarely is that the case during the everyday operation of business in the office. We need to recognize how we can share the power with our subordinates and peers. We can do this by encouraging input from all levels of the organization, particularly from those who will be most directly affected by the decision. Gathering information from many sources often results in synergy, which simply means two plus two may equal five with high quality decision making.

Today, no one person can have all of the answers no matter how smart they really are. Someone else may have the missing link that can make a good decision an excellent one. When I talk about sharing the power I don't mean democratic management or leadership by committee, but just the simple fact of gathering information from those around us. Combine this information with our existing knowledge and the result will usually be a higher quality decision than we could have made with only our own resources and knowledge. We have to be pretty bright to have gotten where we are today. Think how much brighter we will be if we involve our associates with more combined brain power than we can generate alone.

One of the greatest failings of managers today is their fear that if they ask questions, they may be thought of as not having all of the answers. With many of us, not knowing all of the answers may tend to threaten our ego. We are afraid people won't think much of us if we don't have all of the answers. We're the experts, right? The problem is with the growth of knowledge and specialization, no one can have all of the answers anymore. Being an expert today means being able to solicit input. Being an expert today means the ability to deal with and get along with the people you work with. What many managers don't realize is that others really want to contribute to the decision making process.

Watch The Power Dynamics:

To obtain meaningful input, remember that power dynamics are at work and positional power has a great affect on what is said. If you as an administrator, present a problem and then state your ideas first before soliciting a subordinate's opinion, the subordinate's opinion will be invariably influenced by what you have said. You need to present the situation first and then ask for ideas. As people start to talk and comment, it is natural for you to feel the need to comment as they are talking, but fight the impulse. The reason we tend to do this is because we come to the table with more pieces to the puzzle than others do, just because of our leadership position If you talk and interrupt and don't listen, the quality and quantity of input will slow and be influenced by what you are saying.

Never, never ask for an opinion and then demean or deride the information. If you privately or publicly belittle a person's contributions, you can expect nothing from that person again unless, of course, they coincide with your opinions, and those are the opinions you don't want. Those you already have.

As an example to really bring this home: Remember when your boss, the city manager, or the chair of the county board made an arbitrary decision regarding your organization with which you had no input? How did that action make you feel? I can bet that, depending upon the importance of the decision, it caused some real problems! Now, consider how your employees feel when you make an arbitrary decision involving what they do on a daily basis without involving them in the decision. You can bet they feel devalued in much the same way. Now, reverse the situation somewhat and remember when you were involved with the city or county management in providing input into a decision that affected your department. You felt you were a valued part of the process, right? And even if your recommendations were not accepted one hundred percent, after the decision was explained to you, you probably understood the larger issue and could carry on with business.

Everyone responds positively when asked to contribute. This gives them an opportunity to really be a team player. They feel they are a part of the organization. You, as the administrator, win because you have more information with which to make a decision. The employees win because they feel they are really a part of something that is important to them...their job. Contrary to what many people believe, most people really want to accomplish something as they put at least eight hours every day into a profession.

We must realize that no executive is capable of knowing all of the answers. The questions are too complex. You, as the executive, are challenged to guide your agency through what appears to be a future of increased calls for service. You are expected to meet this challenge without the benefits of increasing budgets and personnel.

Solicit your associates' ideas. Listen to what your people have to say. Being a part of and having influence on what affects their lives gives them "ownership" in their agency. This will automatically give you an extra leg up on resources. If your people are given a role in the decision making process, they will expend a lot of extra effort into making sure the process works.

You have just read a book dealing with how people can look at the same issue in many different ways. Realizing this, there should be no doubt in your mind that you can increase the quality of your decision making just by involving your associates in that decision making process. All you need to do is just ask. With input from many points of view, you will not only be surprised at the results, but the overall benefits will be great.

The challenges of the ninety's and on into the next millennium will test us all. As leaders, must take advantage of all of the tools available to us. Understanding the MBTI and the strengths your associates have to offer, can go a long way to understanding the strengths and weaknesses we all bring to an organization. Using this knowledge to our best advantage can give us, as leaders, the ability to continue to move towards the many challenges yet to come.

REFERENCES

Cacioppe, Ron L., and Philip Mock, (1985) Developing the Police Officer at Work. Leadership and Organizational Development Journal. Vol 6., No.5

Consulting Psychologists Press., Inc., Palo Alto, CA 94303. The table on page 14, reproduced by special permission, was taken from Introduction to Type in Organizational Settings. Sandra Krebs Hirsh, and Jean M. Kummerow (1987 and 1990) and is Copyrighted. All rights reserved. Further reproduction is prohibited without Publisher's written consent.

Frisbee, George R. (1988) Cognitive Styles: An Alternative to Keirsey's Temperaments., "Journal of Psychological Type", 16, 13-21.

Gray, Thomas C. (1975) "Selecting for a Police Subculture", in Police in America. Jerome H. Skolnick and Thomas C. Gray, Eds., Boston, Mass. Educational Associates.

Goldstein, Herman. (1977) Policing a Free Society. Cambridge Mass., Ballinger Publishing.

Hanewicz, Wayne B. (1978, April), Police Personality: A Jungian Perspective. Crime and Delinquency.

Hennessy, Stephen M. (1990) "A Study of Uncommon Jungian Personality Types in the Police Profession." Doctoral Dissertation, Dissertation Abstracts International. University Microfilms, Ann Arbor, Michigan.

Henson, Hobart M. (1984) A Study in Police Personality in a Major Police Organization. Unpublished study of the Illinois State Police, Springfield, Illinois.

Hirsh, Sandra, and Jean Kummerow. (1987) Introduction to Type in Organizational Settings. Palo Alto, California. Consulting Psychologists Press.

Jung, Carl G. (1974) Psychological Types. (R.F.C. Hull Translation.) Zurich. Rascher Verlag, (Original Work Published 1921).

Kummerow, Jean M. (1988). A Methodology for verifying type: Research Results. Journal of Psychological Type. Vol. 15.

Lynch, Ronald G. (1986) The Police Manager, New York., Random House.

Manning, Peter, (1976) "The Researcher: An Alien in the Police World", in The Ambivalent Force. By Arthur Neiderhoffer and Abraham S. Blumberg, Eds. Hinsdale, Ill., The Dryden Press.

Macdaid, G. P., McCaulley, M. H., & Kainz, R. I. (1986) Myers-Briggs Type Indicator Atlas., Gainsville, Florida., Center for Applications of Psychological Type, Inc.

McCaulley, M. H. (1990) The Myers-Briggs Type Indicator and Leadership. In K. E. Clark and M.B. Clark (Eds.) Measures of Leadership. West Orange, N. J. Leadership Library of America, Inc.

Myers, Isabel Briggs. (1976) Myers Briggs Type Indicator, Form G. Palo Alto, California, Consulting Psychologists Press.

Myers, Isabel Briggs, and Mary McCaulley. (1985) Manual: A Guide to the Development and Use of the Myers-Briggs Type Indicator. Palo Alto, California, Consulting Psychologists Press.

Rubin, Jesse G. (1974) "Police Identity and the Police Role", in The Police Community: Dimensions of an Occupational Subculture, Jack Goldsmith and Sharon S. Goldsmith, Eds., Pacific Palisades, Calif., Palisades Publishing.

Sanders, Charles B., Jr. (1970) Police Education and Training: Key to Better Law Enforcement. Washington D.C., Brookings Institute.

Singer, June. (1973) Boundaries of the Soul; A Primer of Jung's Psychology. Garden City, N. Y. Anchor Press.

Wilson, James Q. (1985) Thinking About Crime. New York, N. Y., Vantage Books.

Stephen M. Hennessy, born in Hibbing, Minnesota, began his law enforcement career in 1966 as a Special Agent with the Federal Bureau of Investigation in both Houston, Texas, and Newark New Jersey. Steve returned home to Minnesota in 1973 and joined the Department of Public Safety, serving as Director of the Cooperative Area Narcotic Squad in Northeastern Minnesota until 1977, when he was appointed Deputy Superintendent in charge of Investigations for the Criminal Apprehension Division. In 1984 Steve became responsible for the laboratory, information systems, finance, budget, and planning areas of the Division until his retirement in early 1991.

Steve holds a Bachelor of Science in Business degree from the University of Denver, a Master's degree in Public Safety Education and Administration, and a Doctorate in Educational Leadership from the University of St. Thomas St. Paul, Minnesota. Dr. Hennessy presents seminars in the fields of leadership development, team building, prejudice, bias, discrimination, and gender issues and is an associate faculty member of The Arizona State University.

For additional copies of this book, please contact your local book dealer, university book store, or contact the publisher directly. Quantity and educational discounts are available. Visa and Mastercard are accepted by the publisher.

Steve Hennessy offers seminars on the subject of this book, Myers-Briggs and policing, and in the areas of leadership development, communication, team building, prejudice, discrimination, bias, and gender issues.

For further information, please contact Leadership, Inc., of Scottsdale, 7418 East Helm Drive, Scottsdale, Arizona 85260, phone (602) 443-2737.